Winning with Wilkie

A Guide to Better Swimming

David Wilkie with Athole Still

Based on the Scottish Television Series

Stanley Paul, London

Acknowledgements

I should particularly like to thank Athole Still for the very great help he gave me in the preparation of the manuscript, and Dave Haller, technical adviser for the STV programmes, for his invaluable advice on the content. I should also like to thank Tony Duffy and Don Morley for the many excellent photographs which they took specially for this book.

By the same author

Wilkie – an autobiography
David Wilkie with Pat Besford and Tommy Long

Stanley Paul & Co Ltd
3 Fitzroy Square London WI

An Imprint of the Hutchinson Publishing Group

London Melbourne Sydney Auckland
Wellington Johannesburg and agencies
throughout the world

First published 1977
© David Wilkie 1977

Set in Monotype Gill Sans

Printed in Great Britain by litho at
The Anchor Press Ltd and bound by
Wm Brendon & Son Ltd, both of
Tiptree, Essex

Contents

To James,
Best Wishes
David Wilkie

Introduction

More people swim than take part in any other sporting activity, for the ability to swim brings with it rare and varied satisfactions. Everyone can do it – the young, the old, the healthy and the disabled, the lazy and the keep-fit fanatic, the solitary introvert and the gregarious extrovert – and the enjoyment of so many other water sports is considerably enhanced when personal safety is not a constant worry.

Because swimming has a very wide recreational appeal, perhaps the smallest group consists of those interested in organized competition – the swimmers, their parents, coaches and officials. Although I may seem to be well and truly based in this camp, I want to stress at the outset that swimming means much more to me than hours of exhausting training, stopwatches, starting-blocks and races. These things have had their place in the past few years of my young life, but I now look forward to many more years as a recreational swimmer. It is because I have already realized how much the enjoyment and satisfaction increases with improved proficiency that I am writing this book. I would like to help *all* swimmers advance along their aquatic road. My specific aims are as follows.

1. *Sea and sun and me – a scene which I hope will be recreated many times as I become even more of a recreational swimmer in the years to come.*

The recreational swimmer

What I am trying to offer you might best be summed up by the following anecdote which took place only a couple of years ago. I was swimming (purely recreationally!) off an uncrowded beach on the beautiful island of Islay in Scotland. Two small boys were playing in their rubber dinghy which had no paddles and they were obviously frustrated at not being able to propel it. There was, however, a fairly long rope attached to it, so I tied this round my waist and did some vigorous pulling on front crawl, much to the delight of the boys. When I eventually returned to the beach, a man who had been watching approached me and said, 'You must be one of us.' 'What do you mean?' I asked. 'I mean that you're a club competition swimmer, as I used to be myself,' he replied.

Note that he did not say, 'You must be an *international* swimmer.' He recognized only that I swam with a technique proficient enough to stamp me as 'one of us', probably a club swimmer. Now most people like to give an impression of professionalism, even in their leisure activities, and I genuinely believe that you can improve to this extent if you follow the basic instructions in the book and do regular practice. You may not actually become 'one of us', but you can look the part!

The age-grouper

You have already made the choice to become a competition swimmer. This book will help you understand what is required to reach the highest standards. But please consult your coach before blindly following my recommendations. His experience will decide which hints are meant for you; so remember, a good coach is worth much more than any book. Keep swimming.

The coach and top-class swimmer

You will already understand the basic techniques of the four strokes and you will already know the kind of training demanded by international competition. Most of you, however, will not have been fortunate enough to spend four years in the toughest competitive arena in the world – the United States of America. I need scarcely point out that in spite of regular (and sometimes successful) challenges, first from the Australians and in recent years from the East Germans, the American system has always managed to maintain worldwide supremacy. The functioning of that system, and the physiological and psychological preparation required to succeed in it, should be of great interest to every serious student of swimming. I have, therefore, gone into great detail about my experiences in the USA, for I consider they were fundamental in helping me to my major international achievements.

The parent

You may want to coach your own child, or you may wish to be a more knowledgeable observer on your no doubt frequent 'taxi' trips to the swimming pool with your age-group offspring. For the first parent this book should be a useful guide *if no coach is available*, but I strongly advise you to enrol your child with the nearest club which offers squad training facilities. There is no substitute for a good coach and the atmosphere of competitive squad training. The ASA (Harold Fern House, Derby Square, Loughborough, Leics., LE11 0AL. Tel. Loughborough 30431) or the British Swim Coaches Association, (Dormer House, 13 Dormer Place, Royal Leamington Spa, Warwicks., CV32 3AA) will be pleased to advise you on this.

The second parent should remember that his child already has a coach. This book will give you all the background knowledge necessary for an enlightened interest in your child's development, but *try not to become* an 'interfering' parent because of the book. Chose your club and coach well on the basis of past reputation and proven results, then stand back (with interest) and let them get on with it.

Dave Haller, Scotland's Director of Swimming and Britain's most successful Olympic coach, talks to an admiring group of young swimmers.

Athole Still and I give a 'pep' talk to our team before beginning a training session.

1 'Feel'

Experienced swimmers and coaches will no doubt be surprised that I am beginning my book, so to speak, at the end. For the quality known as 'feel' is normally found only in the most experienced, top-class performers. It is that instinctive ability to know just what is right for them, even though it may mean breaking some accepted rules.

In one of his books on that most technical of sports, golf, the great teacher John Jacobs had this to say: 'One of the longest hitters of all time, and one of the greatest amateur golfers ever, was an Irishman called Jimmy Bruen. His feats are legendary, especially "over the water". But if you had seen Bruen swing without a ball, you would hardly have believed the game he played was golf. His action, which included an enormous looping movement, seemed to defy every swing theory known to man.

'Most golfers will have seen Arnold Palmer and Jack Nicklaus, on film if not in the flesh. Palmer's wrists at the top of the backswing are in a position that very few teachers would recommend, and at one time he virtually fell over after every drive due to the way he went through the ball. Nicklaus's right elbow, at the top of his

2. *Bobby McGregor, Britain's greatest front-crawl sprinter – a true natural whose apparently effortless style won admiration throughout the entire swimming world. Here we see his faultless breathing and arm recovery actions.*

9

swing, is well away from the 'orthodox' position. His action is nothing like Palmer's, nor is Palmer's like Ben Hogan's, nor Hogan's like Henry Cotton's.

'How is it, then, that these golfers – and many more like them who seem to have some major flaw in their swing – play such great golf? The answer is simple: whatever they do on the way up from and the way down to the ball, they are 'right' at impact.'

Being 'right' in swimming terms means feeling that the body is in balance and that *your* optimum forward movement is being maintained. Only the swimmer himself can feel that, aided by his own built-in computer specifically programmed for *his* body.

Many of swimming's great names were guided by this 'affinity' with the water into developing new techniques which advanced the sport as a whole. Murray Rose found that he tired quickly when his coach Sam Herford tried to make him adopt the conventional six-beat leg kick in place of his natural four-beat 'balancing' action. The experienced Herford accepted this and Rose began his all-conquering rise to the top. Most of Australia's crawlers followed him, and had such colossal success at Melbourne and Rome that a world-wide reappraisal of front-crawl leg kick took place. Our own Bobby McGregor also had this highly developed sensitivity, which led him to effect one cross-over kick in the middle of an apparently conventional six beat. This is most surprising in a sprinter, particularly in the man who was undoubtedly the world's most consistent 'two lapper' for more than four years. He was never a heavy trainer, so the mechanics of his stroke must have been nearly

perfect – yet unteachable! And so we could go on to many other legendary figures who had great success with unconventional actions – Furuhashi, Jastremski, Saari, Burton, Naber.

I want to make this point early in the book before I have even considered technique, because it is relevant to almost everything that I will have to say about technique. My reader must understand from the beginning that it is impossible to be dogmatic about many of the mechanics of swimming. One can be absolutely specific about the mechanics of a regularly shaped object, like a ship which moves through water with one fixed propulsive action, but not about irregularly shaped human bodies with four 'propellers'. In the ensuing chapters on the four strokes, therefore, after discussing the various techniques (and variations), I will *recommend* the one which follows the most widely accepted principles and which also has a proven record of success.

This does not mean, however, that it should be *imposed indiscriminately* on every swimmer. On rare occasions a coach may come across a young inexperienced swimmer who has an unconventional action but moves efficiently and with an obvious 'feel' for the water. Such natural performers should be handled with special interest and care. Remember that coaches of the stature of Herford, Talbot, Haines and Gambril openly admit how much they learnt from swimmers like Rose, the Konrads, Schollander, Burton. How true is the old adage, 'There are no good teachers, only good pupils.'

I hope I have not overstated these observations, because you will not be confronted by the potentially great 'natural' every day – nor indeed every year! It would be a great shame to ruin him or her in embryo, however, so if as a young coach you have any doubts, take advice from the most experienced coaches available to you.

In general I consider good technique to be the first step towards improving your swimming at every level. No amount of fitness and training can overcome bad faults in technique; I sincerely hope that you will be able to recognize them and eliminate or modify them after reading the following detailed explanation on each of the four strokes.

In the year before the Montreal Olympics I myself made a fairly radical change in my arm action on the advice of my coach. Need I say more?

2 Front Crawl

It is generally accepted that the front crawl had its competitive beginnings over 100 years ago in 1873, when an Englishman, John Trudgen, won a race in London by bringing both arms alternately over the water. Up till then the most popular competitive stroke had been the side stroke, originally in the 1840s with both arms working alternately underwater, and then from the 1850s with one arm being recovered over the water and one under the water. Trudgen's leg kick was completely different from the modern front crawl, as he used an ordinary breast-stroke action. But other swimmers were soon copying his arm movements, partilarly for short races, as the stroke was very exhausting; eventually, by the 1890s, the breaststroke leg action had changed to the scissor-like movement of the side stroke. The next improvement in the stroke came in 1898, when Arthur Cavill, one of six Australian brothers who were all good competitive swimmers, surprised a London audience by beating a well-known champion using a double over-arm technique, but with his legs tied. He did this to prove that the then widely used scissor leg-action might not be the most

3. *Brian Brinkley, England's most outstanding swimmer at butterfly, front crawl and individual medley from 1970 until his retirement in 1976. Here we see how he breathes under the recovering arm, a little later than the other front-crawlers illustrated.*

effective partner of the 'double over-arm'. When he later added a vertical, straight-legged kicking movement, his speed convinced the sceptics and by the turn of the century this technique, which must have been very similar to the modern front crawl, had been almost universally accepted.

Thereafter the front crawl went through several stages, each with its own particular variation. The early Australian crawl, with a two-beat leg kick, gave way to the American crawl, with its six-beat leg kick. This was the stroke with which Johnny Weismuller, the most famous screen Tarzan, dominated world swimming in the 1920s. Then the Japanese further modified the stroke by allowing the shoulders to roll as the arms entered the water. Generally speaking, they kept the six-beat kick; but because of their smaller stature they shortened the length of arm on entry to allow themselves more power on the pull.

At the time of writing all the above techniques are being used in top-class competitive swimming, and world records have been set by all of them in recent years. An obvious dilemma therefore faces those who coach or write about swimming – which particular method should be recommended? I myself favour the American six-beat crawl, and as that technique is still used with the greatest success at all levels, my attachment to it is based on more than mere sentiment. But developments in recent years have shown that, for longer races in particular, a four-beat or even two-beat kick can be more efficient, and I will be saying a great deal about these later on.

Body position

Whichever version of the crawl is used, all coaches and students of swimming agree that the body position should be flat and parallel with the surface of the water. The position of the head can vary considerably – from a very high one, with the water surface at about eyebrow level and the face looking directly to the front, to a very low one, with all except the crown of the head submerged, and the face therefore looking at the bottom of the pool. As a general rule, sprinters carry their heads higher than middle- and long-distance swimmers. The position of the head, of course, affects the position of the hips and legs, so that a high head usually means lower hips and legs, and a low head correspondingly higher hips and feet. The position of the shoulders in relation to the water surface throughout the stroke cycle depends almost entirely on the type of arm action being used. Sprinters usually have the least body roll, and a glance at the strokes of the Olympic 100 metres sprint winners since Weismuller won the title in 1924 amply supports this view. In fact, only Miyazaki (Japan), the winner in 1932, showed any pronounced body roll, although his arm recovery was similar to Weismuller's, and in any case the tremendous success of the Japanese in those Games was due as much as anything to their extremely severe (for those days) training. Now you are no doubt asking yourself which of the body positions will be best for you. I shall return to that subject during my general comments at the end of this chapter, but I do not want to recommend a particular position till we have considered the arm and leg action, both of which influence and are influenced by the overall attitude.

Arm action

The arms are by far the most important propulsive part of the entire stroke. In many swimmers, in fact, the legs may not increase propulsion at all, even though they are kicking. At first sight this may seem puzzling, when everyone knows that it is possible to move quite quickly using legs alone with a float in your hands. We will examine the reasons very fully in the section on leg action, but I make the point now because I want to stress that arms are the thing in modern front-crawl swimming.

To put it at its most simple, the arm action has two main phases: the part out of the water; and the part in the water. Obviously the second phase is by far the more important, because it is then that the forward power is being produced. But the out-of-the-water phase – or 'recovery', as it is usually called – is not totally unimportant. What can be said about the recovery, however, is that a very wide selection of methods can be used, which are all perfectly acceptable and could have little effect on your forward speed through the water. The most common recoveries are:

1. A nearly straight arm taken over high with hand above elbow.
2. The peaked elbow with a slightly swinging action and hand below elbow.
3. The straightish arm taken round just above the surface of the water.

4. *My normal front-crawl recovery. Not many specialist front-crawlers use this recovery, but it feels comfortable to me and all my coaches have accepted it.*

5. *Fellow Olympian Gordon Downie, British record-holder for the 400 metre freestyle, has the most widely used recovery. Note the relaxed appearance of arm and hand in 3, 4 and 5.*

I personally much prefer the second type, but I have seen the other two methods used successfully at the highest level of competition, and I would try to modify them rather than reject them completely, provided my swimmer seemed comfortable with them.

What, then, should be avoided in the recovery? In short, any action which upsets the balance and rhythm of the whole stroke. For example, suppose you have settled into a particular body position and leg kick which is working well in medium-pace practice, but seems to fall apart when you start to sprint. This may well be caused by the recovery. As the arms speed up and work more vigorously for sprinting, they may set up a reaction which causes the body to twist or bounce, and this should be avoided.

The 'working' part of the cycle begins at the moment the hand touches the water in front of the head. The acceptable area of entry is between a line drawn straight forward from the nose and another line drawn straight forward from the outside edge of the shoulder. An entry over the centre line is likely to cause an excessive amount of rolling, and one outside the shoulder line means a loss of time before the hand starts working the water in the 'power zone' – the area between the two shoulder lines, where any propulsive action will produce the most effect. Think of it like this: you are lying on the floor in the front-crawl position with your arms both out in front, and you want to pull yourself forward along one of three ropes placed one outside the left shoulder, one down the centre line of your body and one outside the right shoulder. Which one do you use? Obviously, the centre one, because it is within the 'power zone' in which you can bring your muscles to bear on your levers (arms) in the most efficient manner.

The hand should enter the water nearly flat, with the elbow slightly bent. You may have read or been told that the hand

6.   *Pool-side correction can be very valuable. This young pupil had a tendency to drop his elbow and to allow the hand to enter well outside the shoulder I am telling him always to look at his hand entry before turning to breathe.*

7. *This young pupil is doing a 'head-up' exercise. The pulling arm should never be straighter than as shown here.*

8. *I have never intentionally tried to bend the arm as much as this. It has developed with my feel for the whole stroke.*

should be 'cupped' in order to 'catch' the water, but if, as an inexperienced swimmer, you think of cupping your hand, you will almost certainly 'cup' it far too much. In fact, if you hold your hand absolutely flat with the thumb in and then depress all your fingers about half an inch, you will have the near-perfect position. The hand is your paddle and it is the overall *area* that matters, not the depth of the 'cup'.

As you enter the hand, it may help to incline it very slightly to the outside, so that the third finger touches the water first. This helps to avoid one of the commonest faults in the arm action, namely to allow the hand to drift outside our imaginary line drawn forwards outside the shoulder. Or, to put it another way, with the third finger entering just first, your automatic tendency should be to pull inwards towards the body; this is good, for you are keeping in the 'power zone'. At this point in the stroke we can do one of three things:

1. Press straight down and push back.
2. Press down to the centre line and push out again to the thigh.
   (Both with slightly bent arms.)
3. Press down about a foot, bend the elbow until the forearm almost makes a right angle with the upper arm, and push back with the fingers actually pointing across the body before they finally point down again before recovery.

9. *A side view of the previous photo. Note how the arm has bent in relation to the entering arm.*

As with the various recoveries, all three of these pulling methods have been used with success at the highest level of competition. Most evidence suggests that a technique between the first and second is generally speaking the most efficient and I would certainly recommend either of these two to anyone beginning to learn the front crawl, but one cannot be dogmatic about this. The main aim is to keep maximum pressure on your 'paddle' throughout the pull and the individual physical characteristics and strength of the swimmer will effect the line of the pull.

10. *Here I am indicating the approximate bend of the recommended pull.*

Leg action

Now I come back to my earlier comment that within the full stroke the leg action often gives no propulsion at all. If you swim 25 yards flat out first with your legs tied, then again holding a small float in your hands and kicking your legs, a comparison of the times will make it quite clear that the arms are a very much more efficient propulsive force. Most swimmers take 50 per cent longer on legs alone than arms alone. But using full stroke with two, four, or six leg kicks to each two arm pulls is always at least a little faster than arms alone. It appears that the legs are giving that extra bit of propulsion. This is wrong. The correct conclusion is that the legs are *causing* the extra speed, but not through giving additional power. They assist by balancing the stroke and thereby help to keep the whole body in a position where the much greater propulsive efficiency of the arms can best be used.

If you are still not convinced, just think of a speedboat going through the water at 30 m.p.h. Now imagine that you are hanging on to the end of it kicking like fury. Will it go at 30 and a bit m.p.h.? Of course, it won't. In fact, it will only go at 29 and a bit m.p.h., because your body on the end of it will actually slow it down – your body's top speed at maximum efficiency is far slower than the boat's.

I have laid particular emphasis on the above points because they explain the most important developments in present-day front-crawl swimming. Looking back into recent swimming history before 1956, I now realize that one of the most common technical mistakes was 'over-kicking'

– that is, maintaining a very vigorous leg thrash in the misguided belief that it was increasing the overall speed. The most damaging factor of all, of course, was the disproportionate expenditure of energy, the fuel of the body. Energy is closely related to the intake of oxygen, and all our muscles need oxygen to function properly, the amount required being roughly in proportion to the size of the muscle. Just compare the large thigh muscles with the shoulder muscles, and you can easily see the waste in allowing the huge leg muscles to swallow up lots of oxygen when their power:fuel ratio is extremely dubious.

It must be said, however, that there is still considerable controversy in the swimming world on this point and it is very difficult to reach conclusions on paper. It really boils down to what constitutes over-kicking. I am completely in favour of six-beat kicking, particularly in sprinting, provided that the general 'feel' of the entire stroke is arms-orientated. But whenever there is any indication that the arms are 'waiting for' the legs, that is gliding even fractionally on hand entry (the catch-up stroke drill on page 25 is an extension of this), then we are in an area of diminishing return in relation to effort. I have seen many swimmers at various levels of competition employing actions as described above, but only one achieved genuine world class and that was distance man Hans Fassnacht of West Germany, trained in California by the fine American coach Don Gambril. There seemed no difference between Fassnacht's leg kick on full stroke and when done with a kick board, while all the other superb 'kickers' I have seen, even sprinters like Kornelia

Ender, clearly allow the arms to dominate on full stroke. I, therefore, advise front crawlers to concentrate on a continuous, fluent arm action with the legs 'fitting in' to the cycle.

Provided these factors are well remembered, there is certainly no need to give up doing very vigorous leg-kick practice.

11. *An indispensable part of every winner's training. Excellent for rhythm and fitness.*

Training for legs alone is an excellent part of any programme, particularly early in the season, when it can be an invaluable way of helping to put the body in good condition and getting rhythm into the stroke. In fact, I very often found my 'feel' on front crawl at its very best immediately after doing legs-only practice.

The action itself is quite simple, although there are certain common faults which it is necessary to guard against. The first thing to remember is that, whether you are doing legs-only practice for power, or swimming full stroke and using the legs for position, balance and rhythm, the benefit from the legs can come only if they are in the water. This may seem an obvious point to make, but how many crawlers can still be seen, even in a reasonable class of competition, with their feet coming well clear of the water! Avoid this and the cause of it, which is over-bending at the knee. The whole action, whether you are doing two, four, or six beats is basically a straight leg one. Of course, the knees bend slightly, but this they will do naturally, and it is far better to think of keeping your legs straight than of slightly bending the knee. The inexperienced swimmer who thinks of bending will almost certainly bend too much, and bring the feet well clear of the water.

The depth of the kick varies according to whether you are doing full stroke or legs only. Because they are of secondary importance in the full stroke, the legs should have a very shallow range, with a maximum depth of about 12 inches. If you think of keeping them within the thickness of the body, you will be about right.

On legs only, of course, where they are performing a much different function, the maximum depth is often as much as 18 inches. In both cases, it is advisable to have the ankles stretched as much as possible. It aids streamlining on full stroke and on legs-only the 'whipping' action of a loose ankle on the downward thrash can give good propulsion.

There is also disagreement on whether the main kicking action should be thought of as 'down and behind', rather as if one were trying to kick a football backwards to the bottom of the pool, or 'back and up' with *a very slight* bicycling sensation and the heels just breaking the surface. The first action is much deeper than the second.

I have tried both and believe that if training is done on both methods, the 'correct' kick will *naturally* fit into the whole stroke. Many coaches advise their swimmers to do some leg work with the deep kick (never breaking the surface) and

12. *A nice, vigorous leg thrash, but excessive knee bend has brought the left foot and ankle well above the surface.*

13. *Myself in full stroke showing the near straight leg action. When sprinting, more bend becomes apparent.*

some with the shorter sprint-type kick. I consider it an excellent exercise to do alternate lengths on the two methods.

For my final comments on leg kick I return to the question of timing. Unless I had a 'natural' who seemed to forcefully reject a conventional six-beat action, I would always encourage my swimmers to try to adopt it and most certainly to train on it legs-only. It must be understood, however, that this would not preclude them from racing with two or four beats, if experiments had shown that this timing suited them best on full stroke. This ability to adapt is one of the major landmarks on the way to becoming a really good swimmer.

Many of the world's best swimmers have changed their strokes throughout their careers and some have even varied their action between two, four and six beat, depending on how far they were racing. Roy Saari, of the United States, swam to a world record over 1500 metres using a

two-beat action, and sometimes at the beginning and end of this race he would use a six-beat action! He also used six beats over short distances, where he became one of the world's leading sprinters.

Breathing

This is the only swimming fundamental which we are all doing all the time, and yet for some people it is the most difficult part of the crawl stroke. Now it is probably more difficult to learn to breathe on the front crawl than on any other stroke, but like anything else good practice can make it easy.

Basically, good breathing for swimmers involves two questions: how? and when?

No matter what type of crawl you are using, a turn of the head is the minimum requirement for placing the mouth in a safe inhaling position. If your stroke is properly balanced, your mouth is then in a little trough sheltered by your head and shoulder, and inhalation of air without water reasonably easy. As I said earlier, sprinters as a rule lie flatter with less body roll than distance swimmers, and for them the body position should alter as little as possible during the breath, so that the breathing movement is merely the sidways turning of the head which I have just described.

Some swimmers, however, have considerable body (shoulder) roll, and for them the breathing position is nearly over the shoulder, with the mouth almost facing the ceiling of the pool. Either method is acceptable, but bear in mind that it is not *necessary* to roll the shoulders *excessively*

14. *Two young pupils on deep kicking. One of the best ways of making a swimmer 'feel' the kick.*

21

in order to breathe, and the overriding principle is that the stroke should decide the breathing position and not vice versa.

Breathe in through the mouth and out through the mouth (and nose also if you wish). Once air has been taken and the face returned to the water, most swimmers hold the breath and do not begin exhaling until they commence the head turn for the next breath. I myself hold the breath till immediately before the mouth breaks the surface for the next inhalation. In other words I keep the air in my lungs as long as possible. Most swimmers have fully exhaled just before the mouth breaks surface, as the inhalation time is already very limited and should be used mainly for that purpose. Some, however, finish exhaling immediately after the mouth breaks the surface. It is a matter of preference, but I strongly advise the former.

The entire breathing action can be practised admirably while doing legs only with or without a float. This method is much better than the one often used of standing in the shallow end with the face in the water, because with the kicking exercise you have forward movement, and the same water turbulence you encounter when doing the whole stroke. And also, if you kick hard with those big thigh muscles using up your oxygen you really need to breathe properly!

The best point during the arm cycle to take the breath is when the arm opposite the breathing side has just entered the water and the breathing arm is beginning its recovery. This is by far the most common timing of the breath, although once again we find differences in that many first-class swimmers breathe 'late' – *under* the recovering arm and when the opposite arm is well under the body. Normally, a breath is taken at the same point in each arm cycle, but there are two variations which should be explained: bilateral and breath-holding.

Bilateral refers to the method of breathing after every third arm stroke, i.e. on alternate sides. This method was once very popular until about 1950, but then seemed to disappear from the highest competitive levels of the sport. Over the past ten years, however, it has become quite common again (Bobbie McGregor used it) without ever seriously challenging the popularity of single-side breathing. Bilateral breathing can be an excellent remedial exercise for a single-side breather whose stroke has become a little lopsided through constantly breathing on the same side. A very bad fault of this type can be treated by having the swimmer breathe entirely to the opposite side. These treatments very often stabilize the whole stroke and improve efficiency. They feel awkward to begin with, but those who want to become really competent crawlers must be able to use all three breathing possibilities with comfort. Martyn Woodroffe, our butterfly silver medallist in the Mexico City Olympics had an ungainly, dipping front-crawl action due to instability when breathing. He persevered with breathing on the opposite side and broke British records within a few months.

Breath-holding is much more common, and is used at certain times by many swimmers who are otherwise normal breathers. It consists of holding the breath, usually at the beginning of a race, while several arm pulls are taken, before settling down to normal breathing. The reasons for this are quite simple. The breathing movement, no matter how smoothly it is made, is bound to affect the position and streamlining of the body and therefore slow down its forward movement. It follows that the longer we can do without a breath, the faster we go, and this is why some swimmers – mainly sprinters – do not breathe for the first 20 metres or even more of their race. The great danger, of course, is of holding your breath too long, so that an 'oxygen debt' builds up in your body. If this happens, you will more than lose any benefits derived from your breath-holding. It is very much a matter for the individual, so it is really impossible to advise how long the breath should be held. I use this technique myself when doing front-crawl 'wind sprints', and most leading sprinters do so, but the point always to remember is that normal breathing must be resumed before any discomfort whatsoever is felt.

Conclusion

One thing should be clear from all that I have written about the front crawl: there is no one correct technique. But you should by now have a good idea of the commonest faults and of how to avoid them. You should also now be able to realize why it can be a great mistake to copy a certain swimmer, just because he happens to be successful. The aim of every swimmer should be to make sure first of all that his own natural technique does not have any *major* faults, and then to get on with the hard work and prove that his is 'the' way.

To sum up, in teaching a beginner or learning your first front crawl, bear in mind the following main points, which you will see follow a fairly middle course between the various techniques we have discussed:

1. Flat position with the eyes looking forward and downward (about 45°).
2. Slightly bent arm on recovery, with the elbow pointing towards the ceiling – hand lower than elbow.
3. Fairly flat hand entry between the 'nose line' and 'shoulder line', with arm slightly bent.
4. Press down immediately with the hand and feel that you keep a 'hold' on the water under the body till the hand begins its recovery. The amount of bend on the arm at this stage depends entirely on how you 'feel' the pressure being maintained.
5. Breathe to one side only, once every two arm pulls, and try to breathe by turning rather than lifting the head.
6. Allow the arms to dominate the whole stroke, and keep your leg kick shallow. Experiment with two-, four- and six-beat kicks over various racing distances, to see which suits you best, but I consider that the six-beat is the basic movement. The others are variations of it.
7. Try to cultivate a constant, fluent rhythm.

Training exercises

The following exercises can all be used to improve technique, power or merely to add a dash of variety to training sessions.

Kicking

1. *With float, arms extended*, as already described.
2. *Without float, arms extended and hands locked with one thumb held in the palm of the other hand.* This is an advanced exercise and calls for powerful deep kicking to maintain the body at the

15. *This young swimmer learnt to perform this difficult exercise after only a few weeks of swimming. Her position is a little low in the water, but it will improve with practice.*

surface and drive it forward. The face should be kept in the water and lifted to the front for breathing.

Pulling

1. *With float between the thighs.*
2. *With rubber band round ankles.* A good exercise for the serious crawler, to be done with a faster tempo than normal full stroke.

Full stroke

1. *Head clear of water, shoulders flat, watching hand entry, breathing to front, deep kick.* This exercise is particularly useful in teaching the beginner. The next step can be to drop the face into the water and swim as many strokes as possible lying absolutely flat without

breathing. I have found alternate lengths (or widths) of 'head up' and 'head down' an excellent method of introducing the beginner to the basic body position before adding the breathing head turn.

2. *Single arm pulling*: one arm extended and held to the front while the other does all pulling. Breath is taken to the side in the normal manner every one, two or three pulls. At the end of each length the other arm does the pulling.

3. *Catch-up stroke*: both arms are extended in front and one only completes a pull (with breath to that side) then re-joins the other in front. There is a pause as the legs alone briefly drive the body, then the other arm repeats the process.

Fun drill

The swimmer tries to swim front crawl normally but with one leg bent upwards from the knee, rather like a periscope. The arm action should be very fast with the 'free' leg kicking as in butterfly.

17. *Training thrives on fun like this. Not as easy as it looks. Try it!*

16. *Note the visual control the beginner has over hand entry. To keep the head up she will have to press down really hard and this will develop the sense of 'holding' the water. Compare photo 7.*

E. D. Lacey

3 Back Crawl

The backstroke was for long the Cinderella of swimming. In the past most potential competitive swimmers were drawn to the front crawl as the fastest and therefore most glamorous stroke, or they remained with the breaststroke which was usually the first stroke taught to beginners.

This second-class status of backstroke was probably caused by its early technique which was based on the breaststroke – performed on the back. It consisted of a double arm recovery over the chest and face, entry behind the head, and a double pull round the sides to the hips. This action was married to a single 'upside-down' breaststroke kick. The whole technique, the Old English backstroke, was used in the first competitive backstroke races in 1903.

The first refinement came within a few years with the kick being made to each of two alternate arm pulls, and the stroke finally began to look like the present-day back crawl when the American Harry Hebner added an up-and-down straight leg action in winning the Olympic gold medal at Stockholm in 1912.

Most of the early back-crawlers had a high arm recovery and a fairly deep pull,

18. *Roland Matthes (East Germany) whose near perfect technique has become the model for all budding back-crawlers. Note the steady head position and the very flat shoulder attitude.*

but in 1936 the American Adolph Kiefer won the gold at Berlin and set a new fashion, with a very low recovery, shallow pull, and the arms absolutely straight throughout the action. His method was very similar to that of an oar used by an expert rower in a racing skiff. This technique went unchallenged until David Theile (Australia) won gold medals in the 1956 and 1960 Olympics using a bent arm pull and a 'sitting' attitude with high head and shoulders, so that the body was not flat, but slightly angled to the water.

Most back-crawlers adopted Theile's bent arm pulling modification, but his sitting attitude was generally discarded as being a natural characteristic of his and therefore not to be copied. A flat position was still the accepted one.

Then in the late sixties appeared the man, or rather the sixteen-year-old boy, who put it all together into the definitive, modern back crawl. Roland Matthes, the first of East Germany's many swimming greats, took Cinderella to the ball – permanently. He broke both 100 and 200 metre records many times between 1968 and 1976, setting standards of technique and time as good as anything the other strokes could offer. Even his eclipse at the Montreal Olympics does not in any way detract from his achievements, for after eight years at the top during which he won everything, his motivation in Montreal was very clearly on the wane.

The 'ideal' backstroke which we will examine now is basically the Matthes technique.

Body position

As with the other strokes, a flat position is best for back crawl. If the head is held well back in the water, it is easier to lie perfectly flat, as there is no tendency for the hips to drop. This is a common fault in many back-crawlers and in spite of the success of fine champions such as Theile, I would dissuade my swimmers from using it, unless I felt I had a speedy 'natural', who could not comfortably modify his position. Girls normally have no problems with body attitude, as their better float-ability seems to lead quite naturally to an ideal position. The head should be held *absolutely still* throughout the action and the shoulders quite steady and flat.

Arm action

The arms are the more important propulsive agents, and it has now been scientifically proved that the shallow, straight arm pull is not as effective as the bent arm action. If we consider that the arm cycle begins at the end of a pull, with the hands by the hips, one arm, quite straight, should lift vertically and place itself alongside the head and as near to it as the flexibility of the shoulder joint will allow. In swimmers with normal shoulder joints the arm moves easily through an arc of 180° until just before the hand is about to touch the water and then the mechanism of the shoulder joint causes the arm to drop slightly to the outside and hand

19. *My own high recovery with the palm already turned outward to prepare for the 'catch'.*

20. *My shoulders are particularly supple, so I have no difficulty in placing the arm directly alongside the head without twisting the body to do so.*

entry is made at approximately 11 o'clock and 1 o'clock, where the swimmer's head points to 12 o'clock and his feet to 6 o'clock. Any entry outside these points, at perhaps 10 and 2 o'clock, is unacceptable and a swimmer who cannot comfortably achieve at least 11 and 1 is not destined to be a back-crawler. Having said that, however, there is little premium to be gained by entering at 12 and 12, particularly if the swimmer has to 'over-reach' (alter the lateral position of the shoulders) to do so.

This is a very common fault in back crawl; the main danger lies not so much in the over-reaching itself, but more in what may happen to the hips. Trying to place the right hand unnaturally directly behind the head may cause the hips to move to the right to make the movement possible. If this is repeated on the left-hand entry a constant lateral swaying of the torso results with very detrimental effects on forward movement.

I must stress, however, that I am not

21. *The common beginner's fault of entering the hand actually behind the head. In this case there is a fair amount of hip sway to the left and this should be corrected.*

22. *Right: The most common hand entry position being shown to the pupil. Note the palm already nearly flat as it enters the water.*

against *longitudinal* over-reaching, i.e., trying to lift the arm as high as possible *in its normal arc*, so that the shoulder joint clears the surface before the lay-back for hand entry. This can be a distinct advantage: the large upper arm muscle is above the water throughout the recovery and therefore does not affect adversely the body's streamlining.

As in the front crawl, the hand should 'catch' or 'fix' in the water as soon as possible after contact. Only the palm of the hand can do this, so the swimmer should try to make the initial hand entry with the palm inclined towards the bottom of the pool to assist the catch. Immediately the wrist should rotate so that the palm is inclined towards the feet. We now pull the body past the hand and at the same time the arm should progressively bend at the elbow, till the forearm and upper arm make an angle of approximately 120° as they pass the level of the shoulders. It is virtually impossible to be more specific than this because the right amount of elbow bend varies from swimmer to swimmer. Most of the best backstrokers have more than 110 degrees at maximum bend, but a few have less. You yourself must decide by 'feel'. You should know when you have a real 'hold' of the water – the pressure will be greatest then – so try to keep the pressure up throughout the movement. By experimenting you will find out what is best for you.

An important point to watch once the arm has reached shoulder level is that the elbow should not be allowed to precede the hand. The hand should be ahead of the elbow, so that you feel you are now pressing or pushing rather than pulling.

As the hand passes the shoulder, the swimmer should concentrate on keeping the *full* palm facing the feet – this is possible by flexing at the wrist – and the final push, with the arm straightening itself completely, should bring the hand about six inches below the level of the hip. At this point the palm should immediately turn towards the body, so that the hand will have the least possible water resistance to overcome as it begins the recovery.

23. *The body is still in perfectly flat position as the palm makes an immediate 'catch' on the water.*

24. *This is the approximate amount of elbow bend as the hand passes the shoulder. Note that the full palm faces the receding end of the pool.*

Leg action

I believe that the legs should be subordinated to the arms, as they are in the front crawl, particularly nowadays with the bent arm pull, which is mechanically much more efficient than the Kiefer-type back crawl. I also believe, however, that the back-crawl leg kick does give actual propulsion as well as balance to the stroke, and this seems to be borne out by the fact that all good backstrokers still use an orthodox six-beat kick, as opposed to the wide variety of kicks successfully used by front-crawlers.

The action itself is almost identical with that of kicking a football. As the upper leg drops, the knee bends about 45 degrees to prepare for the very vigorous upward whip, when the real power is applied. At the end of the kick the whole leg is once again completely straight with the instep just breaking the surface.

The foot should be flexed as much as possible with the toes pointing towards

25. At this point the 'pull' has become a 'push' which it continues to the point of release at photo 26.

27. Note the considerable bend of the right leg. This is permissible provided that the kick is flowing from the thigh and the knee does not break surface at any time.

26. The wrist has flexed the hand onwards so that the fingers point towards the feet from under the hips before recovery begins.

31

the receding end of the pool. It increases your ankle flexion to turn the feet slightly inwards, so that if for example you are swimming in the middle lane of the pool, your right foot should kick roughly towards the left corner and your left foot towards the right corner.

Do not make the common mistake of kicking from the knee only. The power must come from the hip, and you can guarantee this if you concentrate on making the knees pass each other. *Neither knee should ever break the surface*, but there should be a space of a few inches between the back of the upper knee and the top of the lower knee when the legs are at opposite ends of the action.

Timing

The coordination of the legs and arms is one which gives complete balance to the whole stroke. As one arm is beginning the pull, the opposite leg is kicking downward. During this same arm pull, the opposite leg will kick upward, and as it commences its second downward action the other arm is ready for the next pull.

It would be very difficult, if not impossible, to learn the timing by thinking about it. One must first practise the arms and legs separately, as indicated in the training exercises, and the coordination of the full stroke will fall into place naturally.

Breathing

It is unusual for a back-crawler to have any difficulty in timing his breathing, for he should be able to do so exactly when he pleases. If a young swimmer cannot easily adopt a rhythm, I suggest that he follows the most common method of inhaling on one arm recovery and exhaling on the other.

Training exercises
Kicking

1. *Arms at side, palms on hips or top of thighs.* Legs kick in the normal manner. Inexperienced swimmers who have difficulty in maintaining a good (i.e. flat) position or reasonable speed may use their hands to scull, i.e. rotate and push the water towards the feet. No arm assistance whatsoever should be allowed.
2. *Straight arms extended beyond the head, hands locked.* This is the definitive back-crawl kicking exercise. The swimmer should concentrate on stretching the arms behind the head, as if trying to pull the body into an absolutely flat position with no dropping of the hips. An exercise for speed, balance, rhythm and position.
3. *Elbows at sides, forearms vertical.* This is an exercise to be used occasionally for deep, strengthening kicking. The chin should be brought forward on to the chest and the swimmer should see that the feet do not break the surface at any time.

A slightly 'sitting' position is advisable, because it increases drag, and the swimmer should work very forcefully on his 'footballing' action. This exercise should not be overdone, in case the low-hipped attitude creeps into the swimmers' normal technique. As a controlled variation, however, it has a valuable part to play in training.

Full stroke

1. *Double arms, normal back-crawl kick.* In this exercise both arms recover and pull simultaneously. The swimmer should try to emulate the normal single arm stroke, but he will undoubtedly have difficulty in finding the normal points of hand entry, as each shoulder joint will be trying to force the other outwards laterally. The swimmer is, therefore, encouraged to lift each shoulder, and so to increase its flexibility.

The double action also necessitates a lifting and stretching of the chest (and therefore of the hips) bringing about a high, flat position. A third benefit may accrue to the swimmer with the very common fault of pulling straight in one arm and bent on the other on full stroke. With both arms pulling simultaneously, he can consciously try to match the feel of the wrong (straight) arm with that of the correct (bent) arm.

2. *Single arm.* One arm is held extended beyond the head and the other arm performs the normal cycle. This exercise is helpful in attaining a stretched, flat position and it induces a swimmer who is inclined to 'roll' to maintain a steady attitude. As with similar exercises on front crawl, several variations of number of pulls, changing stationary arm etc. can be used.

28.   *This is the recommended position for back crawl – long and absolutely flat on the surface.*

29.   *When seen underwater there is still the considerable bend of photo 27 but the knee of the kicking leg is clearly still below the water as the flexed foot barely breaks the surface.*

Pulling

1. *With rubber band holding ankles together.* This is the main back-crawl pulling exercise. The swimmer should concentrate on the same points as in the full stroke, but he will probably find an additional problem in that the absence of a balancing kick will tend to cause a slight lateral sway of the legs/hips. This must be kept to an absolute minimum by great concentration on flat, steady shoulders, 'fixed' head, controlled recovery and even pull.

4 Butterfly

This stroke was the last of the four swimming methods to be accepted for international competition. It originally developed in the 1930s with the addition of the double overarm action to the already established breaststroke. As with the early days of the front crawl, most swimmers thought it too strenuous for anything longer than a sprint, but certainly in short races it proved faster than the orthodox breaststroke. After the 1952 Olympics, however, the two strokes were separated and the butterfly became a stroke in its own right, as it fully deserved, for with the added development of the double up-and-down, fish-tail movement of the legs, the modern stroke no longer resembled the breaststroke in the slightest. Nowadays it is the second fastest of the four strokes, and undoubtedly the most strenuous.

Body position

This must be as flat as the undulating motion of the 'dolphin' kick will allow.

30. *'Mr Gold-medal' himself, Mark Spitz, on his way to the 100 metre butterfly gold medal, one of the seven he won at the Munich Olympic Games. His time for this event was the only world record not beaten at the Montreal Games.*

Arm action

As in the front crawl, the arms are the main source of propulsion, although the legs also give power, much more so than in front crawl. Later we will see that at the beginning of the arm recovery, the second dolphin kick is the only propelling action taking place.

The arms begin their cycle in the forward position, on either side of the nose, but not outside the shoulder line. This is identical with the single arm entry for front crawl, and the similarity does not end there, for the hands also have the crawl position and the arms are again slightly bent at the elbow.

Normally the hands are pressed straight down to a point fairly central under the body, the depth or amount of elbow bend being decided by the strength of the swimmer. One thing is certain, however: a completely straight arm is not efficient, and I personally recommend a considerable bend, before the hands part and the arms straighten for the final push to just outside the thighs. Although I have said that the hands should be pressed *straight* down, one normally finds that to keep a hold of the water each hand will involuntarily execute a near semi-circle before pushing out at the thighs. The underwater action therefore traces a kind of 'keyhole' shape, but I would *not* stress this in coaching. The swimmer should think primarily of 'powering' the hands down and back, maintaining constant palm pressure.

During the recovery there is usually much less of the peaked elbow as seen in the crawl. The arms are straighter and

31. *Note the flatness of the body and the double entry directly in front of the shoulders. The feet are invisible as they are bent upwards ready for the first kick. Compare photo 36.*

32. *This is the point of maximum arm bend in my butterfly. The water is still disturbed after the first kick. Compare photo 36.*

33. *The arms have completed the 'keyhole' with the hands pushing outside the thighs. The second kick just beginning will sustain the body during the arm recovery.*

34. *Extremely flexible shoulders can help the butterflier to maintain a flat position while bringing the arms well clear of the water.*

lower, and whereas I like to think of the crawl recovery as a 'carry' forward of the arm, the butterfly recovery is a much speedier 'fling'. The recovery must be very fast; in the crawl one or other arm is always giving major propulsion, but in the butterfly propulsion almost ceases, and although there has been a kick as the hands left the water the power from this will do well to maintain momentum and body position until the next major surge from the arm levers.

Leg action

The kick is a very vigorous downward 'whip' with both legs working absolutely in unison. It is essential to keep the legs and feet on the same plane, because disqualification results if one foot is even slightly ahead of the other in what could be considered a flutter kick, which is not permissible.

The main points to bear in mind are that the hips should be kept high and that there should not be too much bending at the knees. I want to stress this point on knee-bending immediately because one of the commonest faults of the beginner is to make the kick almost entirely a lower leg movement, often with the feet coming completely clear of the water and 'slapping' down on the surface. The thighs and hips are usually rigid and the propulsive power is nil. The effective kick *must* flow from the hips and the amount of permissible knee bend is in direct relation to the amount of hip lift.

At the highest point in the action the feet should barely break the surface, and at the deepest point the heels should not

35. *The first kick has come just as the hands have begun their 'catch'. Note how the upper body is flat with the bottom clear of the water.*

36. *Considerable knee bend is shown here but when the knees whip downwards the flow will originate in the hips (and upper body) and the seat will come clear of the water. Compare photo 35.*

be more than 12 inches below the surface. Flexible ankles greatly assist the 'whip' in the kick, and it is better to turn the feet slightly inwards in a 'pigeon-toed' fashion to help the ankle extension. As you will see from the above description, the kick is a comparatively shallow one, which allows the body to maintain a fairly flat position throughout the entire cycle.

Timing

After early experiments with one- and three-beat leg kicks to each arm cycle it is now universally accepted that the two-beat is by far the most efficient timing of the legs. The fluency and rhythm of the one- and three-beat actions were never found to be comfortable. The first caused a 'dead spot' in the leg action, the second a slowing of the arm cycle while waiting for the legs to complete their kicks. Both actions,

37. *The inward turn of the feet shows clearly here as the downward kick begins.*

however, have a place in butterfly training as we will see later.

The first kick should be timed to coincide with the entry of the hands, and the second with their final push immediately before the recovery. This timing can be practised simply by standing on the pool side with the knees bent and swinging your arms in the correct butterfly manner. As the arms reach the position directly to the front, straighten the legs, push out the hips and say, 'Kick!' Quickly bend the legs, push forward the hips and, as the arms come to the hips, repeat the process. Eventually you will be able to do this at a fair speed, and you will then have the rhythm of this timing, which is very important to the correct performance of the stroke.

Breathing

The breath is usually taken once in every arm cycle. Some swimmers when racing take more than one arm stroke to each breath, but this is an advanced practice, to be used only by the most fit and experienced performers. Butterfly swimming is one of the most demanding of all forms of physical exercise, and a frequent supply of oxygen is of very great importance.

Having said that, however, I would like to add that I consider it an excellent exercise to sprint flat out without breathing for distances of up to about 25 metres. The absence of any body lift for breathing helps you keep a very flat, and therefore ideally efficient, position, and you will probably find that you can do your fastest times for short sprints in this manner. Only when breathing is fully mastered should you attempt this method with two or even three arm pulls per breath in sprint races (see also comments on front-crawl sprint breath-holding, pages 22–3).

Most top-class butterfliers take the breath late in the arm cycle, where it usually coincides with the second kick and final push of the hands. There are sound reasons for this. The greatest propulsion in the entire stroke comes between the point of entry of the hands and their arrival directly under the body. It is obviously best, therefore, that the body should be in its most streamlined and flat position in order to take full advantage of the power. A breath anywhere in this section, with the inevitable head and shoulder lift, is clearly inadvisable.

The final question to answer about breathing is whether the head should be turned to the side as in front crawl, or lifted directly to the front. Although in the early years of the stroke's development the head turn was favoured, nowadays the forward lift is virtually universal. I feel that this has been brought about naturally by the swimmers themselves, not by coaching. Frankly, I find it slightly uncomfortable to turn the head to the side, and I also find it increases the frequency of unwanted mouthfuls of water.

It would certainly seem that the head turn with no lifting, and the body therefore flatter, should be the most efficient, but it has been rejected. The main point to bear in mind about forward breathing, however, is that ideally only the head should lift, and although it is impossible not to have some raising of the shoulders with the arms commencing their recovery, nevertheless it should be kept to a minimum.

Butterfly is unquestionably the most exhausting of the four strokes, but I consider it to be second only to the backstroke in its technical simplicity, although I know that many will not agree with me. Anyway, I recommend that it be practised very early in any swimmer's career.

Training exercises

Kicking

1. *Hands on scum channel.*
2. *Arms straight, holding float.*
3. *Arms by the side, face in the water.* Try to get hips high and feeling of whole body undulation. Breath is taken to the side every two kicks.
4. *Arms extended in front, hands perform short breaststroke pull to assist the body to dive* just *below the surface.* Two kicks then surface, breathe and repeat.
5. *On the back, arms by the side.* In this position the swimmer can breathe freely and, by keeping the chin hard on the chest, see the action of the lower body. He should concentrate on feeling the very strong thrust and whip backwards of the lower leg with fully flexed feet.
6. *On the side arms extended together, body totally submerged at 90° to surface of water.* In this position the swimmer should try to emulate the genuine fish action, if possible with a feeling of flow and undulation from fingertips to toes. Breath should be taken only when required.

Exercises 2 and 3 should form the mainstay of the competitive swimmer's leg work and all exercises except 6 should be done in the basic two-beat rhythm.

Pulling

1. *Single arm butterfly.* This exercise is very similar to single arm pulling as described for front crawl but with the dolphin kick. One arm remains extended

38. *Beginners should be encouraged to use the whole body in the movement and told not to allow the feet to come clear of the water.*

39. *The feet are at their highest point and as they whip down concentrate on getting the bottom up.*

to the front while the other does continuous normal butterfly pull. The swimmer breathes to the pulling side as in front crawl, and uses a normal dolphin two-beat rhythm. The arms change on alternate lengths.

This exercise brings several benefits. It can be used for *considerable training distances* by comparative beginners and non-specialist butterfliers. It can be used when there is a space problem with several swimmers working out in one lane. The single arm action allows the swimmer to effect a much higher arc than in the normal stroke and this should be consciously aimed at during this exercise. It will help increase the flexibility of the shoulders which is of paramount importance in the full stroke. The greater the shoulder looseness, the easier it is for the swimmer

40. *The water turbulence is caused by my shallow surface dive to submerge the whole body. I stretch forward with the hands and think of the kick as originating in the fingertips.*

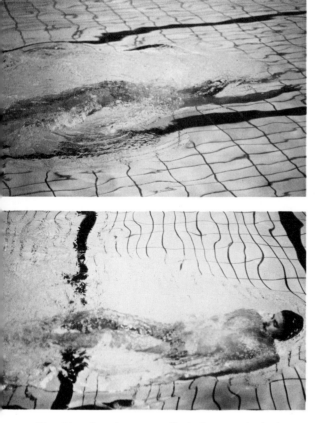

41. *Note how I am actually looking at the kicking movement to check my action.*

42. *This is a wonderful exercise for general body flexibility and I would strongly recommend it to all swimmers, both recreational and competitive.*

to recover the arms clear of the water *without altering the flat body position.*

2. *Arms only (with or without rubber band).* One of the best exercises for inducing hip lift and also, of course, for strengthening the arms. As the hands enter to begin the pull the swimmer should bounce the hips clear of the surface if possible. No attempt should be made to whip the legs, because in this exercise we do not strive for leg propulsion. The legs should remain straight throughout in order to act as a kind of anchor against the arm pull. The timing is one 'bounce' to each pull.

This is an extremely exhausting exercise, but the benefits are such that I would make it one of the cornerstones of my butterfly specialist's training. The idea of 'bounce' in what is essentially a flat action does not appeal to some coaches. It is questioned, for example, by Don Talbot, the great Australian whose butterfly swimmers, Hayes and Berry, took silver and gold medals at Rome and Mexico City respectively. In his book, however, Talbot states that my compatriot Ian Black, had he continued to swim, 'would have become one of the greatest 'fly swimmers the world has seen'. Strangely enough Black did most of his butterfly training on the above exercise! He did not, however, bounce all over the pool on full stroke. What the exercise gave him was great lower back suppleness, power and hip lift. These qualities became invaluable in his high-riding, but essentially flat, full stroke action.

Full stroke

One of the great problems coaching butterfly is that the stroke is so exhausting in its most efficient two-beat form that it is difficult for swimmers, particularly beginners and non-specialists, to use it for normal training distances. There are two stages which a coach can introduce before asking his swimmers to try the competition technique.

43. *At one stage in the development of the butterfly many races took place more underwater than on the surface!*

44. *These pictures show the technique which was used before winners became capable of doing the much more strenuous continuous arm movement.*

1. *Dive butterfly*. As the hands enter the water in front of the face the swimmer lowers the head, bucks the hips and kicks the whole body under water to a depth of about 1½–2 feet. He then continues kicking with the arms extended to the front trying to achieve a genuinely undulating movement from fingers to toes. The number of kicks is optional but I would suggest about six before he planes himself to the surface, does the normal double arm pull, breathes and repeats.

When the coach feels that a certain proficiency has been achieved the kicks should be limited to three or four as a preparation for the next stage.

2. *Three-beat butterfly*. This is done entirely on the surface, but is similar to the dive butterfly in that the arms pause in the forward position while two kicks take place and then pull on the third kick. Incidentally, this is not the three-beat timing used in the early variation of the competition butterfly. In that action the triple kick was partnered by a *continuous* arm cycle. Here the slight pause permits the not yet fully-fledged 'flyer a little gliding rest but makes him amply aware of the demands which the racing technique will soon be making of him.

5 Breaststroke

The breaststroke is almost certainly the oldest method of swimming. It is easy to understand why it appealed to prospective swimmers in ancient times, because its very stable position, with the head always clear of the water, is an attitude that a non-swimmer might adopt naturally when confronted with water. It is certainly the oldest competitive stroke, and indeed was the only one till the end of the nineteenth century, when the front crawl began to emerge. Since those early days the breaststroke has, of course, undergone changes but, unlike the front crawl, there is now almost universal agreement as to what is the fastest and most efficient form of the stroke.

The main characteristics of the old stroke were:

1. Wide, shallow arm pull.
2. Wide, circular leg kick.
3. Long glide after the leg kick, with arms stretched to front.
4. Breath taken immediately the arm pull began.
5. Main propulsion from the legs.

Amazingly this basic technique lasted virtually unchanged for over a 100 years.

45. The feet are about to come together in their final vigorous drive and the arms are already stretching forward to set the body in its most streamlined position to fully benefit from the surge of power.

However it had its problems during that period. In the twenties and thirties many swimmers, particularly the Japanese, took advantage of inexplicit regulations to swim most of the breaststroke races underwater! They did this 'torpedo'-fashion with very long pulls right down to the hips. Then in the early fifties the stroke was in danger of disappearing completely when the butterfly arm action was added to the leg kick with such success that a conventional breaststroker stood no chance in a race.

This final crisis caused the rules to be re-written with such precision in 1956 that they are now more fully and carefully worded than all the other strokes put together. They are as follows:

1. The body shall be kept perfectly on the breast and both shoulders shall be in line with the water surface from the beginning of the first arm stroke after the start and on the turn.
2. All movements of the legs and arms shall be simultaneous and in the same horizontal plane without alternating movement.
3. The hands shall be pushed forward together from the breast, and shall be brought back on or under the surface of the water.
4. In the leg kick the feet shall be turned outwards in the backward movement. A 'dolphin' kick is not permitted.

5. At the turn and upon finishing the race, the touch shall be made with both hands simultaneously at the same level, either at, above or below the water level.
6. A part of the head shall always be above the general water level, except that at start and at each turn the swimmer may take one arm stroke and one leg kick while wholly submerged.

This final standardization of the rules gave coaches the impetus required to restyle an archaic nineteenth-century technique to the demands of twentieth-century competitive swimming and the first to produce a 'prototype' was the great American expert, Dr James Counsilman, coach at Indiana University. His radical re-appraisal resulted in a kind of 'slimming cure' for the old method, in which among other things he encouraged his star pupil, Chet Jastremski, to imagine he was 'swimming through a pipe'. Between them they set a pattern in 1960-1 which virtually all breaststrokers have since followed, with comparatively minor variations depending on the physical characteristics of the swimmers concerned.

With this technique much more power was produced by the arms, and the arm and leg contributions are now acknowledged as being closer than in any other stroke. Indeed there are now almost two breaststroke techniques, one with emphasis on the arms for the 100 metres sprint, and the other with leg emphasis for the 200 metres event. There is so much overlap between the two, however, that I will consider the basic technique and explain the variations as they occur.

Some students of swimming go so far as to categorize arm emphasis as the American technique and leg emphasis as the European technique. At first sight it may seem that there is a *coaching* difference between the two, but closer examination indicates that there is in fact a traditional *body type* difference between those who are recruited to breaststroke in Europe and the USA. For example, I cannot think of a single American breaststroker with a build similar to my own – tall (6 ft 1 in.), slim-hipped, long legs, big hands and feet, and not heavily muscled around the shoulders. American breaststrokers are all of average build with particularly powerful arms and upper bodies but 'normal' hands and feet. This apparent selectivity has, I think, been brought about by the great emphasis put on sprinters in the American inter-university competitions raced in short-course pools. In Europe, however, breaststrokers of my general body build (e.g. Lalle, and luozaytis) have always predominated, but in recent years many medium-build swimmers (e.g. Pankin, Goodhew and Leigh) have appeared, who in general seem to adopt the American method.

There are considerable similarities between the two techniques, however. The difference is basically that the sprinter lies flatter with a slightly wider, shallower leg kick and a more 'fixed' (less movement) head position. Having said that I will concentrate on explaining my own technique, but a swimmer with a stockier build would do well to bear the above points in mind and experiment with his stroke (as I have done) to find which is more suitable for him.

46. *The considerable leg bend on recovery with the feet coming very high (nearly to the bottom) means that the lower body must be slightly angled downwards or the feet would break the surface.*

47. *The 'start' position of the breaststroke. The legs have just come together and the body is surging forward. Compare photo 45.*

48. *This is the deepest point in the pull. Note that I am beginning to exhale through mouth and nose, so that I will be quite ready to inhale as soon as the mouth breaks surface.*

Body position

The swimmer should always think of lying as flat as possible. However, in the case of a 'leg' swimmer like myself, the legs are lower than the trunk and the body is therefore slightly angled to the water, particularly as the legs begin their drive backwards.

Arm action

If we consider the action starting with the arms fully stretched to the front about 2–4 inches below the surface, the first movement is to press both palms downwards and outwards (with arms still straight) to a point about 1 foot deep and approximately midway between the start position and the point at which the hands (if they continued) would be level with the shoulders.

At this mid point the hands start moving inwards (but continuing to press backwards), so that the arms resemble the narrowest point in the butterfly 'keyhole'. The hands are then recovered quickly under the chin (backs of the hands to the

49. *Here we see one of the main differences between the old and the post-Jastremski strokes. In the old stroke the arms would have been straight, nearly level with the shoulders and much shallower, and a fast streamlined recovery was possible.*

50. *The heels have just met after the final push and stretch of the kick. The hands are already moving outwards underlining the 'no glide, continuous power' character of the modern stroke.*

51. *This is the only point at which the heels are wider than the feet. The swimmer should think of lifting the heels up to the bottom.*

front) and the arms stretched fully forward again. The elbows should be kept high and not allowed to come back as far as the shoulder line.

From the starting point, therefore, the fingertips draw two sides of a triangle with a near semi-circle as the third 'side'.

Leg action

Let us consider the kick, beginning with the legs and feet together and extended directly behind the body. The first action is to recover the heels directly upwards and as close as possible to the seat. This brings the knees deep and wider than the feet. At the top of the recovery the feet turn outwards at right angles to the body and wider than the knees, so that the inner edges and ankles of both feet are presented directly backwards. The legs should now feel coiled, ready for a power-

ful release and the breaststroker should feel the soles of his feet 'fixed' on the water, rather like the 'catch' of the palm at hand entry in the front crawl. The kick is really the maintenance of that 'fix' so that the body is forced forwards as the legs straighten and the feet come together with pointed toes.

When I am driving forward on the legs I concentrate on stretching forward and streamlining the body as much as possible.

Breathing

All breath is taken through the mouth alone while the face is looking directly to the front. I exhale as my hands move to the mid-point described in the section on arm action and inhale as they move inwards under the chin (*photo 53*). The considerable leverage of the arms at this point effects a high mouth position well

52. *These back and side views (see photo 46) of the same point in the action, show clearly why the main power in this breaststroke comes from the legs.*

53. *The deep press down and back of the hands has facilitated the high head and shoulder lift for a clear breath.*

clear of the water for an untroubled breath. The head does move upwards and forwards but in a fluent, controlled manner which should not adversely affect the body position.

54. *In the 'old' technique the head would have lifted to breathe immediately the hands parted. Here I maintain a streamlined position.*

Timing

The major development in modern breaststroke, regardless of whether the swimmer is a 'leg-man', an 'arm-man' or a 'fifty–fifty man', is the emphasis on power without pause. The stroke is always 'working' and there should be no dead part in the cycle like the held glide after the kick on the pre-Jastremski version. One of the great American coaches, the late Matt Mann of Michigan University, once said, 'When you're gliding, the other fella' may be pullin'.' He was referring to the once popular glide on front-crawl arm entry, but his saying holds good today for breast-

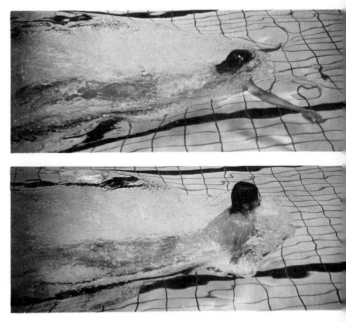

55. *The breath comes late, just after the point of maximum arm power.*

stroke. I concentrate on keeping the stroke moving and start the next part of the cycle immediately the arms or legs have been *fully* extended *(photo 50)*. The timing of breaststroke is difficult and cannot be easily taught by writing about it. Practise the drills explained after this section and you will soon pick up the correct 'feel' of the entire movement.

Training exercises

Kicking

1 *Using kickboard:* in this drill I concentrate on a solid 'fix' of the feet, vigorous drive as the legs straighten and a very speedy 'whip' of the feet together. The head is kept up throughout and I normally hold the feet together for slightly longer than I would a full stroke. It can help to count your kicks to make sure that you are maintaining (or improving efficiency). *(Photos 56, 57.)*

2 *Arms extended with no board:* this is more difficult, of course, and with no board to assist flotability and glide, the tempo is higher than in the previous exercise. Breathing is timed as normally in the full stroke. *(photo 58.)*

3 *Hands clasped behind the back:* this is the most difficult exercise of all. I keep my hands well down over the buttocks and try to touch the heels with the hands (and vice versa). The tempo is very fast and I breathe as I try to make the hands and feet meet.

Pulling

1 *Legs together with inflated tube at ankles — with or without pull buoy.* In this

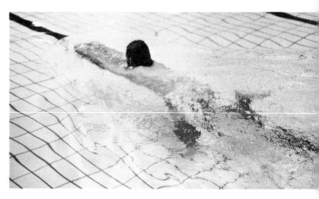

56. *When using a kickboard never let the arms bend. Keep the fully stretched sensation which you should have on full stroke.*

57. *I think the obvious tension of the legs indicates just how much 'whip' and stretch is necessary at this most vital point in the action.*

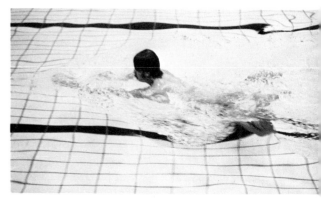

58. *Even without the board it is essential to maintain the stretched position with the hands clasped together and pulling the arms forward.*

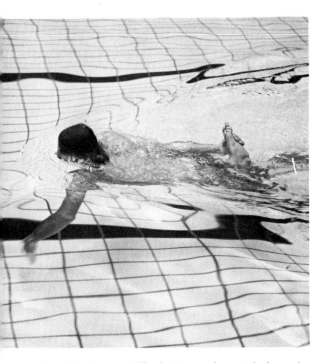

59. *Much more difficult than perhaps it looks and not just for fun. One achieves maximum extension of the long thigh muscles and also of the ankles. The single arm pull is also extremely hard.*

exercise I take two pulls to one breath and the tempo is 'Pull, pull – hold (on extended arms)'.

2 *Legs together with no aids.* There is no 'hold' as above – I concentrate on a faster tempo of absolutely continuous pulling. I lift the head on every pull *as if to breathe*, but I actually breathe only every second stroke.

Fun drill

I *One arm, one leg only.* In this 'fun' drill, I pull my right foot onto my buttock with the right hand and hold it there. I then try to swim normally with the other two limbs. At the end of each length I change over. *(photo 59.)*

Although I call this a 'fun' drill it is very hard work and it also increases the flexibility of the feet and the stretch of the long front thigh muscles.

6 Starts and Turns

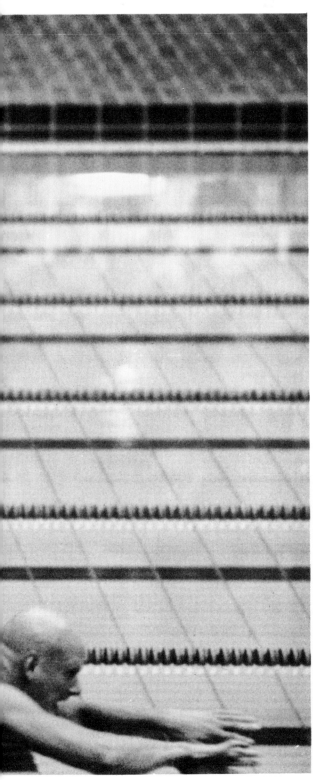

Pat Besford, one of the world's most respected swimming writers, recently described the subject of this chapter as 'the British disease'. I had never quite thought of it in these terms, but on consideration of the improvement in my own performance in these essential skills during my time in the USA I soon realized just how close to the mark she came, particularly in relation to turns. Perhaps, however, she would have been more accurate to call it the non-American disease, for it affects swimmers all over the world except those trained in the United States.

The reasons for this are very easily understood. In the United States, the majority of swimming competitions take place in short-course pools, where the increased number of turns demands that a swimmer be super-efficient to survive in the always extremely competitive atmosphere. In Europe and Australia, the other main centres of competitive swimming, most major events are held in long-course pools and the importance of starting and turning is therefore diminished and traditionally rather neglected. The situation is undoubtedly improving in Great Britain but we still seem to lag a little behind our

60. *The start of the 100 metre breaststroke final at Montreal. Starting nearest the camera Goodhew (GB), Wilkie (GB), Smith (Canada), Hencken (USA), Kusch (West Germany), Lalle (Italy), Iuozaytis (USSR). Woo (USA) is entirely out of the picture. All these used grab starts.*

American rivals. As both these skills are basic to every swimming race, all coaches should insist on regular painstaking practice until a consistently high level of performance is achieved.

The start

The starting rule reads as follows:

1. On a signal from the referee the competitors shall step on to the back surface of starting-block and remain there. On the preparatory command 'Take your marks' they shall immediately take up starting position at the front of the starting-block. When all competitors are stationary, the starter shall give the starting signal (shot, pistol, command).
2. The start in backstroke shall be as stated in Rule 67 *(see pages 58-9)*.
3. The starter shall call back the competitors after first or second false start and remind them of not starting before the starting signal. Such false start, if repeated in same heat (no matter if by same or other swimmer) shall disqualify.

Most of the above is self-explanatory but the following observations from my own experiences may be helpful.

The starter

Most international starters are experienced and first class at their job, but there is always the 'rogue starter' who may not fully implement the 'when all competitors are stationary' clause. If from previous observation you have noted that a certain starter can be intimidated into

giving the signal *because* a swimmer has anticipated the start, find other swimmers who agree with you and lodge a formal protest in advance. I have seen meetings ruined by a poor starter and gold medals almost lost, so do not hesitate in such a situation (admittedly *very* rare) – the swimmmers *must* have confidence in the starter.

The signal

The most common signal is a pistol shot (or similar), but I have experienced a klaxon-

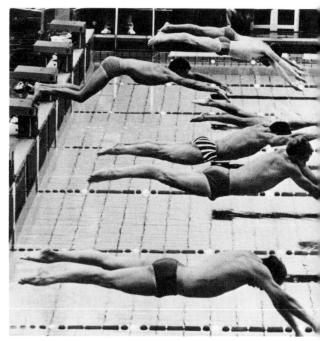

61. *A false start in the final of the 100 metre freestyle at the European Championships in 1966 (Utrecht). The swimmers were not recalled yet it is obvious that the man beyond McGregor (still on block) must have gone early to be in the water so far ahead of the others. McGregor, being next to the offender, knew it was a false start and waited – almost fatally. In fact, he still won – but the camera proves he was right.*

type hooter, so always ask for a demonstration of the starting system at each new venue. At most important meetings nowadays the signal is given automatically directly over each starting-block so that each competitor hears it at the same time.

False start

If there is a false start, you will be recalled by the same starting signal, and a rope will also be dropped across the course about 10 metres from the start. Return to the start immediately, or step down if you

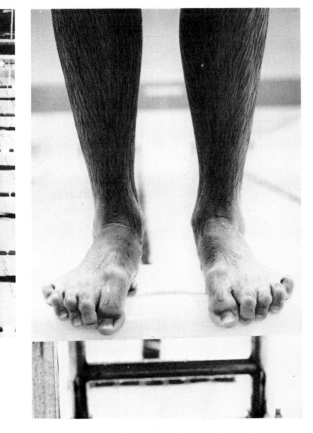

62. *In this shot I am actually standing with my back to the water in order to show a head-on view, but the foot position is, of course, not affected by this.*

did not enter the water, and await the starter's further instructions. I have always considered swimmers who regularly cause false starts at best poorly prepared in their starting techniques, and at worst potential cheats who are trying to gain an unfair advantage. Make sure you are in neither category.

Stance at 'Take your marks'

The feet should be about 6 inches apart, with most of the toes gripping the edge of the block. When standing relaxed, most people have the feet pointing slightly outwards, but in this position only the big toes are able to grip a starting-block, so it is necessary to have your feet absolutely parallel for the correct stance. When you are properly positioned there should be a feeling of real solidity, and when practising you should be able to rock the body fairly vigorously in any direction without overbalancing. In the past the body was usually bent into approximately a right angle at the waist, the arms hanging either straight down from the shoulders or back alongside the trunk, and the eyes looked at the target entry point in the water.

Only in the arm position was there any real difference of opinion among swimmers and coaches, and it was impossible to prove that there was any real advantage one way or another.

In recent years, however, the 'grab' position has definitely become established as the most popular stance (*photo 63*). The hands grab the front of the block with the arms remaining straight. There is considerable bend at the waist and the knees flex

63. *Kornelia Ender (East Germany) four times gold medallist at Montreal, shows the tension and concentration of the grab start.*

sufficiently to maintain a spring-like tension throughout the body.

The dive

On the signal to start, all tension is released, the arms are flung forward and the legs drive forward and upward with all their power. The head is kept up initially, but should drop between the arms, to facilitate a shallow entry, after the body's upward momentum has decreased. This starting technique has led to many swimmers taking up a slightly piked position in mid-air to assist maintenance of height (rather like the hurdle step in the athletics long jump) and provided that the body is completely stretched straight on entry there is apparently an advantage in this. It is a difficult skill to master, however, and improperly executed may lead to the beginner making one of the commonest faults in starting, the 'belly flop'.

64. *The positioning of the hands at the front or at the sides of the block (photo 63) is a matter of personal preference.*

65. *Note the eyes looking immediately at a target spot well down the pool.*

56

This is when the body hits the water, possibly in the correct stretched straight position, but not angled to the water and *with its forward momentum exhausted*. The competitor must then start swimming almost from a dead stop, which is clearly a great disadvantage.

Arms and legs must be together on entry to maintain a streamlined position.

The final point I would like to make about the grab start is that its popularity is not based on personal preference or 'fashion', as were so many starting techniques in the past. Velocity tests were made on a large number of swimmers using various starting techniques and the 'grab' emerged as a clear winner. So if you are not using this method, stop being generous to your opponents and start practising – or invent a better way, for that is always where the greatest satisfaction and success lies.

The pick-up

The speed on entry of a good dive is obviously very much faster than anyone can swim, so do not begin to swim immediately you hit the water. Some beginners even have the legs thrashing before they hit the water, and this, of course, can only hinder your streamlining and slow you down. The exact point at which the stroke 'picks up' the momentum of the dive really cannot be taught – it must be decided by the swimmer himself by experience and 'feel'.

For front and back crawl there are two points to be borne in mind. Firstly, the legs should begin just before the arms; secondly, the body must be completely on the surface immediately after the first arm pull begins. If you find that you are still underwater as you pull, then the dive was not shallow enough.

In butterfly, both at the start and after a

66. *This is the point of maximum height. The body must be stretched out as far as possible.*

67. *Only practice and experiment can decide whether this technique is for you, but it is certainly worth taking the trouble to find out now that titles are decided on thousandths of a second.*

68. *This shows the beginning of my underwater breaststroke pull after a turn, but the technique is identical for the start also.*

69. *Note the depth of the pull and the fact that already the elbows are past the shoulders – a position they never reach on the surface.*

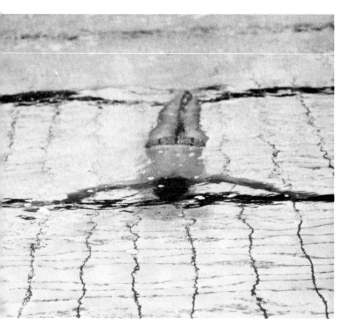

turn, remember that you *must* be fully on the surface after the first arm pull, for disqualification results from a further pull underwater. This rule has been framed to ensure that the swimmers execute the race on the surface and not largely underwater with the diving variation of the stroke. There is, in fact, no advantage whatsoever in remaining underwater for a second arm pull. The breaststroke differs from the other strokes in so far as there is a definite advantage in doing a full stroke of one arm pull and one leg kick under water both at start and turn. The advantage lies in the ability to do a much longer arm pull than is done on the surface. As the dive momentum slows down, the arms begin their pull from the arms-stretched-forward position right back to the thighs. As the arms recover, the legs

give their normal kick, which must bring the swimmer to the surface, for even a part of a second stroke under water causes disqualification.

Backstroke

Rule 67, covering backstroke starts, reads as follows:

1. The competitors shall line up in the water facing the starting end with the hands placed on the starting grips. The feet, including the toes, shall be under the surface of the water. Standing in or on the gutter is prohibited.
2. At the signal for starting, and when turning, they shall push off and swim on their backs throughout the race. The hands must not be released before the starting signal has been given.

70. *The full 'torpedo'. From this position the hands are recovered in front of the body (palms inward) and stretched forward in the normal manner.*

71. *The girls show how it's done in a backstroke final at the European Championships.*

72. *The feet are usually held in this slightly staggered pattern in case one should slip when the main drive is applied.*

3. Any competitor leaving the normal position on his back before the head, foremost hand, or arm has touched the end of the course for the purpose of turning or finishing shall be disqualified.

Much of what I have already said also refers to the backstroke start, in spite of the obvious difference in starting position. The feet are usually placed close together one slightly above the other. The hand should grasp the rail or scum channel, or the starting handles provided at the front of modern starting-blocks, firmly at about shoulder width. On the 'take your marks' pull up into a tense ball with the chin on the knees. This position must be practised a great deal to ensure that your feet will not slip when the big drive from the wall comes, although the slightly staggered

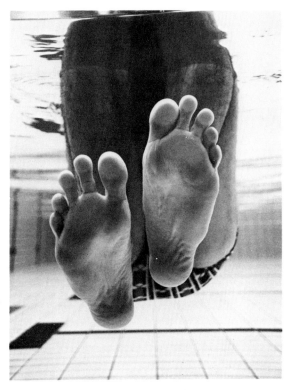

73. *The relaxed position before 'Take your marks'.*

74. *'Take your marks' – the swimmer must keep the feet pressure against the wall rather than downwards.*

placing of the feet should prevent this. On the 'go' push up and out, with the arms flung and stretched straight back and the head between the arms. You must ensure that there is still forward momentum as the arms hit the water, otherwise you will have done the equivalent of a 'belly flop' and for the same reasons.

Two final points on starts. No good starter will give the 'go' till all the competitors are perfectly still, so don't be the one who holds up the whole line by fidgeting. And finally, I advise all beginners to practise high jumps on the spot with toes pointed and legs straight, to get the feel of correct thrusting with the legs. Too many swimmers do not use all their available leg power on the start. The drive required is every bit as vigorous as that needed to push the body straight upwards, and when younger I found jumps on the spot a valuable way of putting the right idea firmly into my mind.

The turn

Just a few years ago any discussion about turns in competitive swimming would certainly have been both lengthy and full

75. *Left: I wish I could do it like this! John Naber (USA) double gold medallist in the Montreal Olympics.*

76. *Mark Spitz looking for the wall to commence his tumble.*

of disagreement. Recently however, there has been fairly widespread agreement as to what are the best methods of turning, even in front-crawl swimming, where formerly about half a dozen turns were in common use.

But before I discuss the various turns I would like to stress that a turn offers a swimmer the chance actually to *gain* time. This fact is often not realized by the newcomer to the sport, who usually sees a turn as a stop and re-start, which must *lose* time, however well performed. This is quite false. Even the obsolete 'grab' and spin turns gain a few tenths of a second when properly executed, and the modern tumble should pick up 0·6 second per turn. The advantage lies mainly in the push-off, because, as with the dive, one can push from the wall faster than one can swim. With the freestyle tumble there is a major bonus in not having to touch with the *hand*, which means that the body can revolve round a point approximately 1 metre from the wall and then push off. But more of that later.

Breaststroke and butterfly

The turns for these strokes are extremely similar, mainly because the rules call for a similar touch by both hands with the body flat on the surface before the turn commences.

The movements of the turn itself are quite logical. As both hands touch (*photo 77*), allow the elbows to bend so that the body as it turns comes close into the wall but without 'kissing it', that is coming so close that the movement becomes cramped as the feet begin to place themselves flat on

77. *Note that immediately the turn has been legitimized by the double-handed touch, the right shoulder is already lifting for the turn. The action is the same at this point in the butterfly/backstroke (and breaststroke/freestyle) transitions in the individual medley.*

78. *The body is already on the side before the feet are properly placed for the push off. Only practice can make these things happen at the same time.*

the wall behind the buttocks. If there is a rail or scum channel, you can pull yourself in and therefore turn faster, but remember that many pools, and certainly inter-national-class ones, have a flat wall, so you must be proficient at turning without using these fixtures.

It is permissible to leave the 'flat-on-the-breast' position, as the time between hand touch and feet leaving the wall during the turn is exempt from the law, and most swimmers therefore do not complete the body turn on the wall. They push off with one shoulder leading, partly on their sides, but are flat on the breast again just before the feet leave the wall. Disqualification results, of course, if the body is still on the side after the push-off.

At this point butterfly and breaststroke techniques differ, for the breaststroke has a complete stroke under water (as at the start), but on the butterfly it is better to surface as the push-off begins to lose momentum. Naturally, the breaststroke push-off is slightly deeper than the butter-fly one, to allow the single underwater stroke.

A forward somersault turn has some-times been used on both these strokes, with a half twist on the second half of the somersault, to bring the body back on the breast before the feet leave the side. It has never really become popular, however; it has a high risk of disqualification. Worse, it is particularly difficult and exhausting to perform with both arms in front of the body throughout the movement. With the alternate arm action of the backstroke and front crawl, however, while the forward arm is leading into the somersault, the other arm is alongside the body balancing it and pulling it through the turn, and this makes similar turns on these two strokes easier and more reliable.

Backstroke

'It is permissible to turn over beyond the vertical after the foremost part of the body has touched, to execute the turn, but the swimmer must have returned past the vertical to a position on his back before the feet have left the wall.'

Backstrokers have always been the most reliable of all swimmers in executing their turns. I am sure that this is simply because they *have* to be efficient, or the result can easily be broken fingers or cracked skulls. Self-preservation is clearly a greater in-centive than mere will to win! The turn in almost universal use is usually called the 'back flip' and consists of a half back somersault followed by a half twist.

As the backstroker approaches the wall he passes under the warning flags about five yards out, and this gives an indication of his position. It is essential that this approach to the turn (and race finish) be practised constantly by the backstroker, because on passing the flags he must also decide which hand will make contact first. This is extremely difficult to estimate accurately, but ideally it should be done without a glance, particularly in a driving finish to the wall where the swimmer with most confidence in his judgement can sometimes snatch victory through a swift, final arm throw.

The hand should aim to touch the wall about a foot below the surface, directly behind the head, and the head and shoul-ders follow it into the beginning of a back

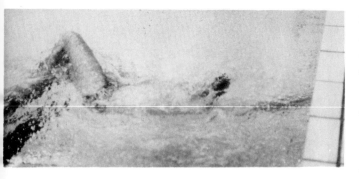

79. *The left hand is reaching down, the legs are already lifting slightly to the left and the head is moving back to the right.*

80. *Legs now well clear and being thrown vigorously at the wall. The right hand will be helping to balance the body at this stage.*

81. *When the feet hit the wall the body will be fully round and ready for the spear-like push off.*

somersault. When the head and shoulders are completely submerged, the body pivots on them, the legs are lifted over the surface, and the feet are slapped on the wall at about the same point as the hand originally touched. The arms are now both stretched out behind, with the head between them, and the push-off drives the spear-shaped body from the wall. Normally, swimmers who touch with the right hand put the head and shoulders back slightly to the left, and the legs therefore come over slightly to the right.

With a left-hand touch, the movements are, of course, reversed. Some swimmers even put the right touching hand down behind the left shoulder, and the legs therefore come over well to the right. I mention these points not to confuse the reader, but to show that provided one follows the basic movements described in the previous paragraph, there will be virtually no effect on the speed of the turn. Whether you put the head and shoulders back to one side or the other, or even dead centre, should be governed to a great extent by how comfortable you feel in executing the turn.

The clarification of the backstroke turn permits the swimmer to turn on to the breast *after* touching the wall. This led to experiments with the backstroke tumble turn, in which the swimmer touched, spun on to his breast, somersaulted into the wall and pushed off already on his back. No leading backstrokers have adopted this turn in competition, because it is tiring, cuts down momentum into the wall and is not significantly faster than the back flip. I am in favour of practising it during training, however, because executing skills of this type is an excellent way of developing general 'watermanship' which increases confidence in body control in any turn.

Front crawl

'In freestyle turning and finishing the swimmer can touch the wall with any part of his body. A hand touch is not obligatory.' The front crawl has seen a greater variety of turns than all the other three strokes put together. In the early fifties, however, the 'tumble' turn was introduced in America for sprint races, and gradually its use was extended to middle-distance events. Since about 1964 it has been used universally by men and women for all distances. The advent of this turn has been the greatest single cause of the improvement in front-crawl turning in recent years for it is so much faster than any of its predecessors that swimmers now realize that they must tumble well to stay in the race. Moreover, in the original tumble the swimmer still had to touch with his hand, but now 'any part of his body' – the feet – complies with the rule and that amendment in itself caused the world freestyle records to be re-written.

The tumble consists of a forward somersault straight into the wall with a half twist during the final part of the somersault and the beginning of the push-off, to bring the body back on the breast. It is not an easy turn to do well, and the young swimmer must persevere with his practice in order to become fully proficient.

In learning any very fast movement, such as a golf swing, it is better to concentrate on a few main points and then practise constantly to iron out any imperfections.

It is very easy to confuse your brain by trying to think of too many things at one time, and the result is nearly always disaster. With the tumble, the basic movements to concentrate on are as follows:

1. When the leading hand is about one foot from the wall, thrust the head downwards and forwards and at the same time lift the hips (photo 82).
2. Keep the legs fairly straight and fling the feet at the wall as your body is beginning to turn on to its side during the last part of the somersault (photo 83).

82. *Here we see just how much the tumble has reduced the times in freestyle. The turn is executed nearly a metre from the wall so that the race length is in effect cut by nearly 2 metres.*

83. *It is possible to see here that already the body is turning on its side and the full soles are being presented to the wall.*

84. *Note how the left arm is pushing upwards towards the surface in order to increase the speed of spin.*

85. *The final position before the push off. On the stretch away from the wall the body will complete the final quarter turn to bring it into the breast.*

3. Use the arms to stabilize and increase the speed of the somersault *(photo 84)*.
4. Bring the hands together and push off with the feet in the same position at which they hit the wall *(photo 85)*.

If you are a sprinter, it is essential to be able to turn with either hand leading, so practise with both. In middle and distance swimming, however, it is quite easy to adjust the stroke slightly, so as to reach the wall always on the same hand.

Only experience will teach you how far from the wall to commence the turn, but you must be close enough to ensure a good bend at the knees for the push-off.

If you experience a need for breath when turning on the non-breathing arm, it will hinder you little to snatch another breath before you go into the wall. This is much better than being in distress on the push-off and having to surface early.

The whole action should be smooth and continuous, and if you think of yourself as a rubber ball hitting a wall then you will have the right idea. Beginners can best practise it by doing *complete* forward somersaults when in full stroke in mid-pool. This will give them the feel of spinning fast and using the arms to assist. They should do the same at the wall to practise judgement of distance from the wall. Then back to mid-pool to practise the somersault and the final half twist. And, of course, finally practice and more practice will put the whole thing together on the wall at varying speeds.

Team race starts

Only the lead-off man in a team race does a normal start while the other three swimmers have 'flying' starts. The advantage of a 'flying' start lies firstly in the elimination of the reaction time between pistol shot and the swimmer beginning to move, and secondly in the fact that the team swimmer may be well into his dive, but *with his feet still on the block*, when the incoming swimmer touches home. As much as 0·7 second can be gained by a really superb take-over, and no properly trained swimmer should be satisfied with less than 0·5 second.

If we study the six finalists in the 1976 Olympic individual 100 metres breast-stroke who also swam for their countries in the medley team finals we note the following improvements: 0·61 (Henken), 0·62 (Wilkie), 0·64 (Kusch), 1·67 (Smith), 0·04 (Lalle). Only Iuozaytis (USSR) was slower (0·18) and his performance and Smith's were obviously the result of fluctuations of form not connected with the flying start.

The ruling has always been the same, in that the out-going swimmer's feet must still be in contact with the block when the in-coming swimmer touches the end of the course. In the perfect take-over, therefore,

86. *A relay take-over at the World Championships in Colombia in 1975. Note the fixed concentration of the nearest swimmer on his incoming team mate. See how the swimmer on block 6 is already going but with his feet still on the block, although his team mate has not yet touched.*

the hand touches and the feet leave the block simultaneously. In the days before electrical timing, there was constant controversy about dubious take-overs, because the body is always well over the water before the feet leave the block and it was so easy for a judge to form the impression that the swimmer had gone early. Nowadays electrical timing systems govern both touches and take-offs, so there is no possibility of error.

Most swimmers dispense with the grab start for take-overs and concentrate entirely on these things:

87. *The right arm (unseen) is moving behind the body as the legs are moving under to present the feet on the wall.*

89. *Even before the leading arm has touched the body is preparing to turn to that side.*

90. *After hand contact the swimmer is fully on his side and the head is already moving out again.*

88. *Left: The body is now nearly fully on the back and the arms are coming together above the head for the normal backstroke push off.*

1. Judging when to initiate their dive (usually when the in-coming swimmer is about 1 metre out).
2. Maintaining contact with their feet until they *actually see* the hand touch.

Once again it is a question of practice makes perfect, but a swimmer should never forget the special responsibility which he bears in a team race. It is bad enough to let yourself down by a mistake, but much worse to fail your colleagues. Make sure you are not the one who wants to crawl off to a solitary corner after a disqualification.

The final point to remember on take-overs is that in-coming swimmers also have a particular responsibility. They must hit the wall *clearly with no glide* over the last metre, for their waiting colleague will already be moving on the block and may not be able to adjust his take off to any change of rhythm or mis-touch on the part of the finishing swimmer.

Individual medley turn transitions

The individual medley expert, as befits his title 'the complete swimmer', must be skilled in all turns, including three not found in single-stroke events. They are as follows:

1. Butterfly to backstroke
2. Backstroke to breaststroke
3. Breaststroke to freestyle

The first and third transitions are very similar to a normal butterfly (or breast-stroke) turn in that, after the double handed touch, one shoulder leads back out of the turn (photos 77, 87). When moving on to backstroke, however, the swimmer places his feet on the wall in a more horizontal alignment (photo 88) to permit the normal backstroke push-off.

The second transition is also best executed by allowing one shoulder to lead into the turn (photo 89) and the other to lead out (photo 90) always bearing in mind that the body *must* be on its back until the leading hand touches. This transition offers the swimmer the opportunity of doing a full back somersault which will bring the body into a position ready for a push-off on the breast. Some individual medley swimmers use this, but I always found it too tiring and not conclusively faster than the normal turn. I leave that decision to you.

7 The Structure for Champions

A glance at the current world record lists will show that there are two main centres of swimming excellence, East Germany and the USA. Any search for the road to the top should begin with an examination of the success of these two countries, in order to establish what is relevant to each of us, be we swimmer, coach, club president, national association official or Minister of Sport.

In East Germany the state has artificially re-located all outstanding sportsmen in five well-equipped centres, and in the United States the best sportsmen gravitate naturally (sometimes artificially, if sports scholarships are 'artificial') to the large number of traditional universities and colleges which also offer excellent facilities. Once this concentration has been achieved, although by different methods, there are considerable similarities in the preparation of the sportsmen concerned. Each system provides what I consider to be the five most important ingredients for success at international level and although I know it is difficult to duplicate them exactly I strongly recommend that everybody reading this, whatever their capacity, should try to come as close as possible to these ideals.

91. Here a Japanese squad typifies the group unity and co-ordination of a training session. The swimmers are almost certainly watching a large training clock to know the exact second at which their next repetition must begin.

Group training

Nowadays the training required for competing at international level is long and arduous. If it is done alone it seems doubly so. Working in a group engenders rivalry (friendly or otherwise) and the normal interplay of differing personalities. These factors undoubtedly alleviate the exhausting demands of training, for the swimmer involuntarily becomes involved with his colleagues instead of constantly thinking of himself, his own problems, his own fatigue, his own times. There may be those who for a variety of reasons cannot train with a squad and I would not want to discourage them, for this is a quite common problem within the present structure of British swimming. Take heart from the performances of Britain's former swimming captain Brian Brinkley. He carried out a great deal of his very tough training alone and he warrants the highest admiration for that fact alone, apart from his managing to achieve an outstanding international ranking. Not many have Brinkley's singlemindedness, however, and I would suggest that a journey to join a good squad is more likely to pay dividends than ploughing a solitary furrow in a nearby pool.

Availability of facilities

This is a self-evident prerequisite of becoming a swimming champion, but there are a few points I would like to make regarding the amount and quality of the required facilities.

First of all, I do not consider it necessary to train constantly or even regularly in an Olympic size (50 metre) pool and in my view swimmers who make long journeys *solely* for that reason are adding unnecessary difficulties to the already hard job of training. There are in fact many disadvantages of training only in a 50 metre pool. Firstly, the sheer size tends to depersonalize a training and coaching session, diminishing the inter-relationships which were described as so important in the previous section. In a small pool the coach will often give instructions to both ends of the pool from a point midway along the pond side and in this way *everybody* is *always* involved in what is going on, even though an instruction may not be specially directed at him. I really believe this helps take the pressure, physical and psychological, off each individual swimmer.

Secondly, small pools mean higher tempos, faster times and turns (page 62) and it is very good to get the 'feel' of that additional speed, which can serve as a target for training and competing long course. The majority of American training and competing is done in short-course pools and the performance 'carry-over' into the long course is there for all to see. In practical terms, I believe that a well-trained and fit short-course swimmer should adjust to long-course swimming within a dozen sessions. So don't fret if you have only a 20 yard tank at your disposal, just work conscientiously and you will have nothing to fear in long-course training, which you should consider as an occasional, interesting, helpful and necessary adjunct of your normal training.

Whatever the quality of your facilities, they should be available for a minimum of twelve hours weekly and at this low figure I would expect only an extremely talented 'natural' to make any impression at international level, and then only at sprint distances. A more realistic availability would be twenty-four hours weekly, for a twice daily two-hour stint with one day's rest seems normal around the world.

Before I go on to discuss training loads in these periods, I want to make it quite clear now that I am *totally opposed* to young age-group swimmers (8–14) making anything like that commitment to swimming. Four hours of work-load is for the mature (17+), top-class performer, who has slowly built up to that level. I attribute a significant part of my own achievements to the fact that I was 17 or 18 (and not stale from 7 or 8 years of huge work-loads) before I began training twenty-four hours weekly.

We all now know that it is *possible* to produce world-class swimmers between the ages of 13 and 15, but the 'drop-out' rate of these swimmers before they reach their true physical maturity is very high indeed. In my view it is far better to limit training and competing considerably until the swimmer is approximately 14 years old. From that age to 17+ the loads can be increased according to the aims of the swimmer. As a general rule I would recommend the following training spells

92.　*It's all too much for 14 year old Jenny Turrall (Australia.) Believe it or not, she's just won 800 metre freestyle in a new world record!*

for the various groups (assuming a hard commitment throughout most of the session):

8–11 years　1 hour daily
11–14 years　1–2 hours daily
14–16 years　2+hours
16+　　　　as required.

I have intentionally overlapped each group because there can be a variation from swimmer to swimmer and coach to coach. The over-riding principles *must* be that the kids are enjoying it, want to do it and that progress is being made by *emphasis on good technique*. If a young swimmer produces world-class times within these criteria then it's nobody's fault!

Motivation to train and compete

Very little would ever have been achieved in life if someone had not felt motivated to take up a challenge. This desire is particularly important in advanced forms of physical training, where participation often entails pain, both physical and psychological, and the acceptance of a life-style which can seem monk-like to the outsider.

The first motivation must come from within the individual himself, but it can be given impetus in a variety of ways.

The group

There should be a calculated effort made to impress upon each swimmer that they belong to and are welcomed by the group (squad, team, club) and that the group

itself is 'special'. At the University of Miami we had team track-suits, a team name (The Hurricanes), a team 'war-cry' and before competitions we entered the pool through a smoking hoop! It may seem like a circus act, but it was fun, we felt 'special' and there was great motivation to make the team. This type of incentive can be further developed within the group by having graded squads and costume flashes for achieving certain performance standards.

Travel

This is one of the most basic incentives of all, for most people have a great desire to travel and the young are no exception. The atmosphere within a club really sings if there is an interesting trip in the offing and many swimmers actually think more of the excitement of visiting another part of the country or even another country, than of the swimming itself. This is perfectly understandable and in its way a good thing, for it helps to take their minds off the fatigue and hurt of hard training.

Swimming is very fortunate in this respect, for its worldwide network of clubs gives countless opportunities for exchange visits which permit youngsters to see the world at an age when most of their non-swimming friends will still be reading about it.

93. *The very happy group of Britons at Miami University in 1976. Fellow Olympians Paul Naisby (left) and Sean Maher (right) with Scotland's Sandra Dickie. We were part of a big, happy swimming family under Coach Diaz.*

There is much to be gained by these trips in the competitive sense also, for they help swimmers to learn about their own reactions to being away from home for extended periods: how they compete, train, sleep, eat, travel, react to team-mates, react to meeting people. All these are important if they are to reach to highest levels of the sport where they will have to overcome any weaknesses – and cope with the pressure of representing their country.

Of course trips cost money, but group travel is not expensive nowadays and hospitality or hostel accommodation can usually be arranged. At Miami we raised funds for our annual winter training trips by jumble sales, raffles, and such like and each swimmer subscribed only about £30 personally. In this way we visited Jamaica, Puerto Rico and Colombia in successive years. Since returning to Britain I have seen extremely cheap inclusive holidays advertised for the December–January period to places like Majorca, Ibiza and North Africa and I feel sure that a very reasonable deal could be negotiated at a hotel with swimming pool for a training trip during that period.

International representation and major championships

All the incentives we have discussed so far are available to most reasonable competitive swimmers but the ultimate incentive will be within reach of only a few. This is the honour of representing your country in an international match or at one of the major championships – the Olympic

On the scoreboard:

FINA

Hird-Brown 00:00.0

1 GOLD DAVID WILKIE
SCOTLAND

4 SILVER BRIAN BRINKLEY
ENGLAND

7 BRONZE GARY MACDONALD
CANADA

94. *Two of the great incentives which keep most swimmers training hard – representing your country in a far off land. Here we see the pool at the Commonwealth Games, New Zealand in 1974.*

Games, World and European Championships and Commonwealth Games.

All squads should be constantly reminded of the possibility of reaching the top and it is a great help to have a former or current champion visit a club to coach or demonstrate.

Once a swimmer has achieved performances which make international representation clearly possible, no further motivation should be necessary. If it is necessary, however, then the swimmer clearly has a psychological problem which the coach will need to examine with great care.

Professional coaching

The coach is the most important single factor in producing top-class swimmers – more important even than the swimmers themselves, for the ideal coach will organize and inspire even undistinguished pupils to performances that might have appeared beyond their ability, while the undistinguished coach will surely fail even with gifted pupils. Any examination of consistent success in most sports will simply corroborate this – but among British coaches we have the examples of Dave Haller at Southampton and Cardiff, Derek Snelling at Southampton and Vancouver (Canada) and in the United States the late Bob Kiputh of Yale University, Doc Counsilman of Indiana University and more recently Mark Schubert of Mission Viejo,

California. Other countries show similar examples.

The coach should be father, doctor, psychiatrist, teacher, confidant, entertainer and general 'fixer' to his charges. The great coaches make light of difficulties and still produce the champions.

As I have set such a high standard for the ideal coach you will all now want to know where to find him. Unfortunately I must say immediately that he will be extremely difficult to find in Britain. That is not meant as a criticism of our coaches, but more of the structure of swimming (and amateur sport in general) where the opportunities for a coach to work in a professional manner are extremely rare. Most of Britain's coaches are either semi-professional or wholly amateur, and with the best will in the world, their commitment to their pupils inevitably falls short of the ideal, because their job and domestic demands on their time prevent them from gaining the full-time experience necessary to learn this particularly difficult profession.

The champions from the USA and East Germany (and until recently Australia) were *all* trained by full-time swim coaches. Britain undoubtedly has the coaching talent and indeed the same traditional university structure as the United States, but unfortunately our educational system apparently does not consider it worth while to have a full-time coach at every major university and college throughout the country. Until we have government intervention to redress this situation, the British amateur sportsman aiming for world titles will probably have to relocate himself to one of the very few coaches in Britain who are able to operate fully professionally. Many swimmers have already done this in their search for excellence and at the time of writing some seventeen have gone further afield to American universities.

Indeed I recently read a major article in a Sunday newspaper on the fact that British diving is in a depressed condition because there is no full-time coach 'to coach the coaches'. Such is the state of British amateur sport.

Before finally leaving the coach, however, I must record my wholehearted support and gratitude to the many semi-professional and amateur coaches in this country, for without them the sport would collapse. There will always be a place for them, for even in an ideal structure they have a valuable contribution to make as assistants to a full-time head coach.

A well-organized competition programme

The confidence of an entire squad or individual swimmer can be shattered by competitive demands for which they feel unprepared. At the beginning of each training year every swimmer and coach within a training structure should know the major objectives for the year. The aims of every competition leading up to these peaks should be well understood and reasonable targets set for the period. Even a defeat can be shrugged off successfully by the swimmer who knows that he has not 'peaked' and that the race was only a planned stepping-stone towards the 'big one'. But more of this important subject in the next chapter.

8 Training in America

I was already an Olympic silver medallist when I arrived at Miami University in January 1973, so why do I credit so much of my success since then to the American system, when it may seem probable that I would have continued to improve in Britain? There are a variety of reasons for this, the first of which does not reflect great credit on myself. Frankly, I had great difficulty in motivating myself to continue training, for in the year before the Munich Olympics I did not seem in any way a potential finalist let alone a medallist, and a future in British university swimming made no appeal whatsoever. Fortunately for me, Frank Thomas, the coach at Warrender Club in Edinburgh, persuaded me to continue. I was selected for the British team and in the twelve weeks before the Games, working in a top-class squad, I put in more training mileage than ever before. My silver medal was as unexpected as it was in many ways undeserved, because of my uncommitted attitude in late 1971 and early 1972. My appetite for gold had been well and truly whetted, but at the same time I realized that it could never be satisfied if I remained in Britain and wanted a university education. I therefore gladly accepted an athletic scholarship at Miami University and found

95. *The swim complex at the University of Miami. Myself with Coach Diaz, senior of the three coaches to the swim squad.*

all the essentials which I have already discussed in the previous chapter. When I stood on the block for the 200 metres breaststroke at the Montreal Olympics I had put behind me three and a half years of the kind of training I had had for only three months before Munich. I had tempered myself psychologically through four dual meet seasons, four National Collegiate Athletic Association (NCAA) Championships and four Amateur Athletic Union (AAU) Championships, which match anything in the world for high-powered competitiveness. In Munich I was an outsider with no pressure on me. In Montreal I was a hot favourite with all the pressure on me and I came through. These things I feel I owe to my time in the United States.

In the States they work on the basis of a two season (or two peak) year lasting from the beginning of November till the end of August. The first season leads up to the NCAA championships (at the end of March) and the AAU Championships (in mid April), both short-course events. The second season culminates in the AAU long-course championships, World Championships, Pan American Games or Olympic Games, usually in late August.

First season

At Miami our usual training loads, all on a 25 yard course, were as follows:

November Relatively light work after hard summer season. Average 8000 yards per day.
December Real beginning of heavy winter training with a minimum load of at least 12000 yards per day. Towards the end of this spell is a two week stint of between 18000 and 20000 yards daily, usually done at the training venues described in the previous chapter.

January The dual meet season begins now. This is the series of matches against each other university in the 'conference' of your own university. We had a match at least once a fortnight leading up to the NCAA Championships at the end of March. On average each round trip is about 1500 miles so we normally travelled on a Friday (by air) and raced on a Saturday. Each swimmer can have as many as three events in the $1\frac{1}{2}$ to 2 hour meet.

These matches are obviously excellent stepping stones towards the championships, but we made no special preparations for them. Training continued on a daily basis of 10000 to 12000 yards and the only 'rest' was the day of travel before the event.

February Continuation of training at 10000 to 12000 yards level. Technique was stressed in an effort to eliminate any inconsistencies which may have showed in the initial competitions in January.

March Now begins the 'taper', the final preparation towards the big NCAA Championships meet, which is usually held on the last three days of March. Training was cut down considerably from week to week:

Week 1	10000 yards daily
Week 2	8000 yards daily
Week 3	6000 yards daily
Week 4	4000 yards daily

The six to seven days before the beginning of the meet is the true taper. Basically we did the bulk of training in 25 and 50 yard sprints on our speciality strokes. These sprints would be evenly divided between fast, high-quality work (95 per cent effort) with two to three minutes rest and slower repetition 50s with only ten seconds rest. In these two ways we achieved speed and maintained good heart and lung efficiency without exhausting the muscles unduly.

On the actual day of competition we did some very easy swimming to warm up, then a few only very hard 25s and 50s at racing speed. Thereafter we concentrated on keeping warm, eating sensibly and relaxing.

In many respects the taper is the most important part of a swimmer's entire preparation, for if it is badly carried out the previous several months of training will have been wasted. The general principle should be the three R's (to use Dave Haller's expression). The swimmer must be rested, relaxed and rehearsed. Beyond that it is difficult to lay down hard and fast rules, because a taper is a very individual preparation and coach must adapt his taper to the amount of work carried out and the mental approach to training and competing of each swimmer under his charge.

Within two weeks of the NCAA Championships, we had the AAU Championships. Many of the same swimmers would again be competing for what was in fact the American national championships, but they always seemed an anti-climax. The team spirit engendered in the American university system is such that one feels much more motivated and excited in representing one's college at the NCAA champs than oneself at the AAU champs.

The comparatively short time between these two big meets poses the problem of whether to maintain a taper or train up for a week and re-taper the second week. I preferred to extend the taper swimming 6000 yards the first week and repeating the true taper the second week.

Typical American winter training sessions

For explanatory notes to the training sessions which follow, see page 84.

November

First session
500 yard loosen swim front crawl and back crawl
1000 yard as 10 × 100 yard individual medley (no rests)
5 × 100 yard kick on 2 min. (personal best approx. 1 min. 07 sec.)
15 × 100 yard individual medley on 1 min. 45 sec. (personal best approx. 54 sec.)
500 yard work on stroke technique

Total for session 4000 yards

Second session
900 yard swim as
  25 yard butterfly
  50 yard back crawl
  75 yard breaststroke
  100 yard freestyle
  125 yard butterfly   (approx. 60 per cent
  150 yard back crawl effort)
  175 yard breaststroke
  200 yard freestyle
5 × 200 yard individual medley on 4 min. (personal best approx. 1 min. 50 sec.)

20 × 50 yard own stroke on 1 min. (personal best approx. 27 sec.)

20 × 25 yard underwater swimming (good exercise for heart and lungs) approx. 75 per cent effort

6 × 100 yard freestyle on 1 min. 30 sec. (personal best approx. 46 sec.)

Total for session 4000 yards

Total for day 8000 yards

December

First session

1500 yard kick, pull, full stroke alternating each 100 (front crawl or back crawl)

10 × 400 yard freestyle on 4 min. 45 sec. (personal best approx. 3 min. 46 sec.)

8 × 200 yard own stroke on 3 min. (personal best approx. 2 min. 01 sec.)

4 × 100 yard freestyle on 1 min.

Total for session 7500 yards

Second session

16 × 50 yard freestyle on 50 sec. (personal best approx. 22 sec.)

4 × 400 yard individual medley on 5 min. 30 sec. (personal best 4 min. 04 sec.)

8 × 200 yard front crawl pull with inner tube and pull buoy on 3 min. (personal best approx. 2 min.)

20 × 100 yard front crawl on 1 min. 15 sec.

800 yard drill work (different variations of your own stroke)

Total for session 6800 yards

Total for day 14300 yards

January and February

First session

4 × 375 yard on 5½ min. front crawl (personal best approx. 3 min. 30 sec.)

5 × 125 yard on 2 min. 15 sec. front crawl (personal best approx. 1 min.)

5 × 175 yard breaststroke pull on 3½ min. (personal best approx. 2 min. 10 sec.)

10 × 25 yard front crawl without breathing on 30 sec. (personal best approx. 10·3 sec.)

9 × 50 yard freestyle on 40 sec.

50 × 400 yard kicking on 6½ min. breaststroke (personal best approx. 5 min.)

300 yard swim down (relaxing off) any stroke

Total for session 6000 yards

Second session

700 yard swim mostly front crawl and back crawl

10 × 50 yard kicking on 1 min. breaststroke

5 × 200 yard individual medley (reverse order) on 3 min. 15 sec. (personal best approx. 1 min. 52 sec.)

6 × 200 yard on 3 min. breaststroke

10 × 100 yard on 1 min. 40 sec. (alternating fast and slow) front crawl

2 × 50 yard for speed breaststroke

Total for session 5000 yards

Total for day 11000 yards

March

4 × 100 yard on 1½ min. descending (taking each one faster than the previous one and with the final one flat out) front crawl

6 × 50 yard on 1 min. descending front crawl

100 yard swim front crawl

4 × 50 yard breaststroke on 1 min. descending to 100 per cent effort

1 × 200 yard breaststroke broken by 10 sec. rest at each 50 yard (all out, with three pulse checks every 30 sec. after finish)

100 yard swim easy front crawl

3 × 200 yard freestyle, negative split on 3 min. 15 sec. (personal best approx. 1 min. 45 sec.)

100 yard swim down

Total 2000 yards

Second season

After the AAU championships I usually took a rest of two to three weeks although I did some swimming every day, the amount and quality depending entirely on how I felt. In May we began summer training outdoors in a 50 metre pool. (Summer distances are therefore in metres.) We were fortunate in having this facility at Miami, but many American swimmers continue to train mainly short course with no adverse effect on their eventual long-course competitive performances.

May. The daily total was about 8000 metres done as in November. This may seem a not unduly heavy load for swimmers still quite fit, but the main college examinations come in mid May and as the vast majority of American men swimmers go to college, training commitments are kept to a minimum.

June and July. Really heavy training recommences with schedules totalling 15000 metres daily. Any small meets are taken in one's stride with no taper whatsoever.

August. Commencement of the taper.

Week 1   10000 metres daily
Week 2   7000 metres daily
Week 3   4000 metres daily
Week 4   4000 metres daily

The final taper up to the big event (American outdoor championships, World Championships etc.) is the same as previously described.

Two typical summer training sessions

First session

1000 metre alternate butterfly and freestyle
6 × 300 metre freestyle on 5 min. (personal best approx. 3 min. 05 sec.)
8 × 100 metre kick on 2 min. (without board) breaststroke
8 × 100 metre pull on 1 min 30 sec. with ankles tied by rubber tube front crawl (personal best approx. 1 min. 10 sec)
30 × 50 metre front crawl 10 sec. rest after each 100 metre swim down
10 × 100 metre own stroke on 2 min.

Total for session 7000 metres

Second session

500 metre swim (just to loosen down)
5 × 200 metre individual medley on 3 min.
10 × 50 metre underwater swim (allowed 2 breaths per length) on 1 min. 30 sec.
6 × 400 metre kick on 7 min. breaststroke (personal best approx. 5 min. 50 sec.)
16 × 50 metre as
    4 × 50 butterfly on 1 min. (personal best approx. 27·5 sec.)
    4 × 50 backstroke on 1 min. (personal best approx. 28 sec.)
    4 × 50 breaststroke on 1 min. 10 sec. (personal best approx. 30 sec.)
    4 × 50 freestyle on 50 sec. (personal best approx. 24·5 sec.)
800 metre pull own stroke
8 × 100 metre butterfly and breaststroke on 2 min. (each 100 split one length butterfly then one length breaststroke)
3 × 400 metre individual medley (each 400 with a different stroke order)

Total for session 8000 metres

Total for day 15000 metres

Notes on the training sessions

The work loads given are basically for a middle-distance swimmer. The pure sprinter would do slightly less and the distance swimmer slightly more.

Each week there should be one rest day.

On race day most top swimmers 'shave down' for their event. They remove all exposed body hair (even from the head) in an effort to increase body streamlining by reducing drag. The effect of this procedure is very difficult to prove conclusively. What is certain, however, is that the ritual of shaving down can give a psychological boost to the swimmer, for among other things the feel in the water is quite exhilarating when shaven.

When the schedule states a time e.g. 'on 2 min.', it means that each repetition began every 2 minutes *including* swimming time.

In all repetitions the aim was to do approximately the same time for each one or possibly improve slightly ('negative splits'). It is bad pacing to produce erratic splits or to show a constant increase in timings.

After each set of repetitions with frequency, I have given my approximate personal best time for the basic distance. This will give you some idea of how to calculate your own frequency. In the November first session, for example, I did 5 × 100 breaststroke kicking on 2 min. with a personal best of 1 min. 07 sec. If your personal best for 100 kicking (on your own stroke) was, say, 1 min. 40 sec. (about 50 per cent more) your frequency would be on 3 minutes (50 per cent more than my 2 min.). By trial and error you will then find the time you can repeat.

The warm-up swims were usually done as a mixture of front crawl and back crawl with a little butterfly.

When doing drill work we never did consecutive drills on the same stroke, but always interspaced drills on other strokes.

Pulse-taking is a very valuable method of discovering how a swimmer's fitness is progressing. We used it at least once or twice a week throughout the season. At peak of fitness I usually had a 40 per cent drop-off 30 seconds after maximum effort (200 beats to 120) and a further 25 per cent on the minute (120 to 90).

9 Land Training

I believe that the vast majority of the champion swimmer's training must be done in the water. There are considerable advantages, however, in complementing this with land-work to improve strength, endurance, flexibility and general fitness. Swimmers much appreciate the opportunity of staying out of the water yet continuing to improve their efficiency in a different environment.

The most common forms of land-conditioning are as follows:

1. Calisthenics
2. Circuit training
3. Exergenie (a type of portable pulling machine)
4. Isometrics
5. Pulleys
6. Weight training

I used all these forms of training throughout my competition preparation (except the taper period) for an average half an hour each day. At Miami we regularly rang the changes of the type used and it would be impossible within the confines of this book to list the considerable number of variations we covered.

The average swim coach is not an expert in this field, and many of them turn to one of the many excellent specialist books on the subject so that they can present a wide variety of work to their swimmers.

Only with regard to weight training need I offer a word of caution, for here over-enthusiasm can cause serious damage.

No swimmer should indulge in these exercises without specialist advice or supervision. As a general rule we never used weights of more than 40kg and did high repetitions e.g. 3×15 for endurance. Only our male sprinters and butterfliers used heavier weights (70kg) with fewer repetitions (3×5) to build the strength especially required for these events.

In none of the above land-work did I follow schedules which were in any way unusual or uncommon. There are, however, certain other exercises which were specially recommended to me by Tony Power, the British team physiotherapist, and I believe that they have been of particular benefit in my physical and psychological preparation for competition.

In 1974 I had damaged three intervertebrae discs in the upper spine and the pain often made it difficult for me to train and compete. Tony Power massaged and manipulated my back until I felt quite fit again, but he then suggested that I try some exercises based on the classical yoga postures. These movements emphasized alternate stretching and relaxation and had to be done with great concentration and attention to the breathing rhythm. After trying them for only a short time I found myself feeling so 'poised' physically and mentally that I adopted the habit of performing them before most of my training sessions and the first three before all my major races. They are as follows:

Exercise I   Starting position – lie in 'press-up' position.

Push head and shoulders up and back as far as possible.

Bend one foot towards back of head.

Twist head round to look at foot. Rep using other foot.

Exercise 2

Sit with soles of feet together, pull feet into crotch; breathe in stretch up, back straight; lean forward breathing out; breathe in stretching up and back. *Repeat 5–10 times.* On the last attempt, try to stay down with head very low for 10 seconds.

Exercise 3

Sit with knees bent, arms outstretched at either side.

Repeat 5 times to each side

Place your right leg under your left thigh.

Now step over your right knee with your left foot.

Grasp your left ankle wi your left hand. Taking your right hand behind your back, inhale and twist to the right side so that you are looking bac over your right shoulder

Repeat whole sequence 5 times.

end both feet towards back of head.

Twist head to right to look at feet.

Twist head to left to look at feet.

exercise 4

Kneel with knees apart; hands behind back on feet. *Push hips forward, hold for 10 seconds.*

Exercise 5

Sit with right leg out straight, other foot in crotch; hold ankle; breathe in – look up.

Breathe out, head down on knee. *Hold for 10 seconds.*

Change legs over. *Repeat.*

ace your right hand on our left thigh and left and around your waist. hale, twist to the left de. Breathing out, return o the first position.

10 Aids and Equipment

Fortunately swimming is not a sport requiring expensive equipment – that is another of its many attractions – but there are a number of items which can help swimmers who want to improve. The most common are the following.

Pulling aids

Several kinds are available.

A small polystyrene board is clasped between the upper thighs. This type can also be used for kicking drills.

One or two polystyrene tubes joined by rope are tied loosely round the thighs.

Rubber inner tube is slightly inflated and tied round the ankles. It is used either alone or with a pull buoy.

A 2 or 3 inch wide section of a car tyre inner tube is placed round the ankles. This is a very difficult pulling exercise, but can be extremely beneficial, particularly for sprint work, as the great drag from the legs forces the swimmer to speed up the arms and adopt a high flat body position.

Hand paddles, oval 'pancakes' of plastic about 9 by 6 inches with finger holders, bring increased resistance to the pull to strengthen the arm and shoulder muscles, but they can also help the beginner to assimilate quickly the 'feel' of catching and holding the water.

Kick boards

The most popular ones nowadays are made of polystyrene and can be any size from about 12 by 9 by 2 inches to 20 by 12 by 1 inches.

Goggles

There is now a large selection of small goggles available which give excellent underwater vision for seeing turns and opponents two or three lanes away. Their main use, however, is probably in protecting the eyes from the sometimes annoying effects of chlorinated water and in recreational swimming. I grew so attached to mine that I always wore them in competition also. They are also available by prescription for swimmers who normally wear spectacles.

Rubber caps

Many male competitors carry their hair closely cropped or even shave bald in order to eliminate drag in the water. If a boy (or girl) wants to retain a long hair style however, I think a cap is a much more sensible way of tackling the problem than reluctantly removing the hair. I myself like my hair long and I have found it no drawback to wear a thin elastic cap, which I recommend in preference to the heavier rubberized type.

Swimming trunks and costumes

I am sure there is no need to tell most swimmers of the excellent lightweight racing apparel which is now available to them. There are many advertisements which already do that. But it can be an advantage, both actual and psychological, to have a heavier suit for training. Many champions do this, or regularly wear two suits, so that they feel lighter and more streamlined when they don their 'special' suit for competitions.

Drag suits

These are specially designed costumes (trunks for males also) which are of heavier material and incorporate open pockets for catching the water. The aim, of course, is to increase water resistance and therefore to help strengthen the swimmer. I myself have never worn one, but they are very popular with many swimmers and coaches. Provided that they are not used excessively, they can bring variety to training.

Ear plugs

Many swimmers suffer from *otitis externa* which is a mild (but painful) inflammation of the outer ear, caused by the water carrying infection into the ear. If a swimmer has recurring bouts of this (as I have), I recommend ear plugs of the wax-ball type as opposed to the already-shaped rubber plugs. A perfect fit can be made with a wax plug, which can be retained for several uses. Wax plugs may sometimes work loose and allow some water to penetrate, but in general I have found them extremely helpful and I unreservedly recommend them.

Nose clips

There was once a fad for using nose clips but it quickly disappeared and nowadays very few leading swimmers are seen wearing them. However, there are occasions, particularly on a backstroke turn and push off, when it is very difficult even for an experienced swimmer to prevent some water entering the nose. If your nose is particularly sensitive, therefore, it may be beneficial to wear a clip. Try to bear in mind, however, that it is preferable to keep mouth and nose clear at all times.

11 Winning the Race

If you have turned to this chapter of the book first, hoping to find one magical 'Wilkie' secret for winning races, I must immediately disappoint you and advise you to go back to the beginning and read the whole book, for my best secrets have already been exposed there. What I would like to do in this chapter is to examine the various factors which make a few sportsmen winners and so many others 'also-rans', and to discuss my own thoughts before my two biggest races: the breast-stroke at the Montreal Olympics and the individual medley final at the AAU Championships in April 1976.

For me the winner is the one who can bring together at a given moment the three essential criteria for success in competitive sport. They are as follows.

Physical and technical preparedness

I hope this has already been fully covered throughout the book but my final word must be to urge you always to be completely conscientious in training. If you cheat, even occasionally, those moments are the ones you will remember when the pain of a race is beginning to make itself

116. *The occasion when everything had to come right for me – and did. The 200 metres breaststroke in the Montreal Olympics.*

felt. Believe me, nothing is more satisfying than standing on the starting-block knowing that you have a backbone to take you through the race – not a wishbone. Without the correct attitude to his race and his opponents, a sportsman cannot expect success, no matter how well prepared he may be physically.

I have been fortunate in that I have usually managed to achieve my optimum, or very close to it, when I have wanted to and have been in a physical condition to do so. This, in fact, may be due to a natural characteristic of my personality, but I have nevertheless consciously cultivated a pattern of behaviour directed towards success. When I realized after the Munich Olympics that I really could be the best in the world, I thereafter refused to consider not being so. I was absolutely positive in all my thinking and planning for major events, and although I sincerely hope I was never arrogant, I did try to exude an air of relaxed confidence, particularly when 'on view' to my major rivals. A good coach helps foster this attitude throughout his entire squad and in this respect I was particularly lucky with Bill Diaz at Miami. If my confidence was a bit of a pose when I first came under his control, he was as much responsible as I was myself for converting the pose into reality.

The American swimmer (and athlete) receives considerable help towards this attitude by the structure and nature of the

117. *Myself with Mark Spitz at the World Champs in California, 1975. At Mexico City in 1968, the schoolboy Spitz seemed one of those who failed psychologically to measure up to their physical capabilities. Perhaps his greatest achievement was in persevering for a further four years until Munich, where he showed just how much determination he had.*

competitions available there. There is so much racing at such a high level that psychological 'hang-ups' are usually ironed out pretty quickly. There are so many outstanding performers that virtually no one finds himself under the kind of pressure of public expectation that bedevils a star in smaller countries. Every Olympics highlights examples of outstanding sportsmen who are well-prepared physically but cannot approach their normal performances 'when the chips are down'.

It is very difficult to offer advice to a sportsman in this position, for even the world's greatest psychiatrists often find it impossible to decipher the workings of the individual psyche. I would just say this. First of all make sure that everything which is completely under your control is absolutely right (training, tapering, tactics) and compete as often as possible at the highest possible level, giving 100 per cent all the time. If you have the swimming ability, you will win a lot of races: perhaps not all of them, but you will be breeding a reputation as a competitor and every opponent you ever meet will feel that reputation sitting heavy on *his* back when the 'big one' comes along.

And one final point. Do try to have a major interest away from the sport. Everybody needs to relax some time, but if you are constantly thinking of races, titles, times and opponents, you will always be under some kind of pressure. Pressure leads to tension and tension is a killer.

Tactics

There is no doubt that tactics are not as important in swimming as in some other sports such as athletics, where man-to-man confrontation can involve rapid changes of pace and actual shoulder-to-shoulder involvement. But there is no less doubt that a poorly thought-out race invites defeat.

Before all races a swimmer should know his own, and his opponents', strengths and weaknesses. He should also have a very secure idea of the pacing of the race. The longer the event, the more important the function of pace, but even in a 100 metre sprint I believe that pacing is important, because no swimmer can give absolutely 100 per cent from start to finish. I know that some swimmers say that they go 'flat out' from the gun, but if this were really so, then the half-way split for all sprint champions would always be their fastest ever 50. It seldom is; if one looks at the American 50 freestyle records, one finds that *somehow* the record-breakers always manage to squeeze off an extra 0·1 or 0·2 second in the individual 50. I believe that any swimmer who really did 'swim a 100 as a 50' would lose double his first length gain on the second length. In my sprint races with John Hencken I knew that he had to go out very fast and try to 'hang on' down the second length against my superior stamina and better finish. I was therefore usually content to try to stay very close up, using him as a hare, and then attempt to win the race down the second. This had been successful against Hencken at the AAU Championships at Long Beach before the Olympic Games. At Montreal, however, I added another strategy to this and fostered the impression that I was concentrating entirely on the 200 metres and would let the 100 metres look after itself. I therefore swam within myself in the heats and semi-final, but unfortunately miscalculated the ability of the young Canadian, George Smith, and found myself in lane 6 for the final. With John as fastest qualifier in lane 4, my normal strategy against him became virtually impossible, because I could not see him properly down the first length. In the actual race I allowed Hencken to get too far ahead (0.97 sec.) at 50 metres and left myself an impossible task on the second length.

In retrospect I regret my attempt at gamesmanship. In the heats and semi-final I should have showed the American that he had a fight on his hands and been at my normal place alongside him in the final. Who knows what effect it might have had on him? It was my own decision, however, for I had discussed it with no one, and I may have paid dearly for it. But I must make it quite clear that I take nothing from Hencken's victory, because to win as he did with world records in heat, semi-final and final, was nothing short of magnificent.

The entire episode strengthens my belief in the policy which I have advised in the previous section – there is no gamesmanship quite so effective as winning races in personal best times.

I had this very much in mind in the final of the 200 metres at Montreal. I was the fastest qualifier by nearly three seconds and I had Hencken where I wanted him, immediately on my right. I was finished with fancy gamesmanship and I aimed to win in the same manner as I usually did, by letting him set a fast pace to the 100 and then moving away from him thereafter. It was simple, straightforward and uncomplicated and for most swimming races that is the best way.

One exception to this is the individual medley event, in which there can be many tactical variations. I specialized in the 200 metre version and I must admit that my victories in this event have given me special pleasure, because most experts consider the individual medley man as the complete swimmer.

I always warmed up and did some fast work on all four strokes in the race order (butterfly, backstroke, breaststroke and freestyle). I then practised the turn transitions in the same order.

In spite of the commonly held view that over 200 metres the fit swimmer should be close to flat out the whole way, I never did, but preferred to rely on a simple philosophy:

1. Stay as close to the field as possible on your weaker strokes.

2. Put on the pressure on your stronger strokes, and

3. Have *something* left for the final freestyle leg.

I concentrated exactly on this in the 200 final at the American AAU Championships in 1976. Unlike my breaststroke races, where only Hencken offered serious rivalry, in this final there was an intimidating line-up of at least six potential winners. In that situation it is particularly important to know all your rivals' strengths and weaknesses: someone may do so unexpectedly well on one stroke that you must alter your own race plan to stay in touch.

Fortunately for me only a minor change was made to the pre-race plan. Coach Diaz had told me to stroke the last few metres to the wall without breathing, but frankly I was so exhausted that I had to ignore his advice and breathe. Thankfully I still won and was only 0·17 sec. outside the world record.

In Conclusion

Swimming has given me so much that I could not possibly do justice to it in one book, but if what I have written encourages you to accept the challenges of this great sport, then I will have achieved something. The cornerstones of your hopes should be self-discipline and determination and, believe me, these factors can more than make up for not having webbed feet!

I hope that you have enjoyed reading the book and that you have learned something from my experience (and my mistakes!). May I leave you with this thought – a performance which seems impossible today will be commonplace in a few years time, so why wait? It's up to you.

And a final thought to the recreational swimmer. Even modest improvement in your technique will help you enjoy your sport more, and that must be the aim of all sports at all levels. Keep practising and be at home in the water.

118. *Montreal, 24 July 1976. My greatest satisfaction!*